Women in the Arts

WOMEN in the ARTS

Nina Simone

He who neglects the arts when he is young
has lost the past and is dead to the future.

—Sophocles, *Fragments*

WOMEN in the ARTS

Nina Simone

Kerry Acker

Introduction by
Congresswoman Betty McCollum
Minnesota, Fourth District
Member, National Council on the Arts

CHELSEA HOUSE
PUBLISHERS
A Haights Cross Communications Company
Philadelphia

CHELSEA HOUSE PUBLISHERS

VP, NEW PRODUCT DEVELOPMENT Sally Cheney
DIRECTOR OF PRODUCTION Kim Shinners
CREATIVE MANAGER Takeshi Takahashi
MANUFACTURING MANAGER Diann Grasse

Staff for NINA SIMONE

EDITOR Patrick M.N. Stone
PRODUCTION EDITOR Megan Emery
PHOTO EDITOR Sarah Bloom
SERIES & COVER DESIGNER Terry Mallon
LAYOUT 21st Century Publishing and Communications, Inc.

A Haights Cross Communications ◀ Company

www.chelseahouse.com

First Printing

1 3 5 7 9 8 6 4 2

Library of Congress Cataloging-in-Publication Data

Acker, Kerry.
  Nina Simone/by Kerry Acker.
    p. cm. — (Women in the arts)
Includes index.
Contents: Nina at Carnegie Hall—The prodigy, 1933-1944—The concert
pianist, 1944-1954—The chanteuse, 1954-1959—The star, 1958-1962—
The activist, 1963-1966—The high priestess of soul, 1967-1969—The
expatriate, 1970-1978—The diva, 1978-2003.
  ISBN 0-7910-7456-0 (hardcover)—ISBN 0-7910-7952-X (paperback)
  1. Simone, Nina, 1933- —Juvenile literature. 2. Singers—Biography—
Juvenile literature. [1. Simone, Nina, 1933- 2. Singers. 3. African
Americans—Biography. 4. Women—Biography.] I. Title. II. Series:
Women in the arts (Philadelphia, Pa.)
ML3930.S553A2 2003
782.42164'092—dc22
                                                         2003016578

Table of Contents

Introduction

Congresswoman Betty McCollum
Minnesota, Fourth District
Member, National Council on the Arts

I am honored to introduce WOMEN IN THE ARTS, a continuing series of books about courageous, talented women whose work has changed the way we think about art and society. The women highlighted in this series were persistent, successful, and at times controversial. They were unafraid to ask questions or challenge social norms while pursuing their work. They overcame barriers that included discrimination, prejudice, and poverty. The energy, creativity, and perseverance of these strong women changed our world forever.

Art plays a critical role in all our lives, in every culture, and especially in the education of young people. Art can be serious, beautiful, functional, provocative, spiritual, informative, and illuminating. For all of the women in this series, their respective forms of artistic expression were a creative exploration and their professional calling. Their lives and their work transformed the world's perception of a woman's role in society.

In reading this series, I was struck by common themes evident in these women's lives that can provide valuable lessons for today's young women.

One volume tells the story of Coco Chanel, the first fashion designer to create clothing for women that was both attractive and utile. Chanel was one of the first women to run a large, successful business in the fashion industry. Today, it is hard to imagine the controversy Chanel stirred up simply by making women's clothing beautiful, comfortable, and practical. Chanel understood that women wanted a sense of style and professionalism in their fashion, as men had in theirs.

Chanel's extraordinary success demonstrates that we should not be afraid to be controversial. Even today, women of all ages worry far too much about stepping on toes or questioning authority. To make change, in our own lives or in our community, we need to stand up and speak out for our beliefs. The women of this series often defied convention and ruffled some feathers, but they never stopped. Nina Simone sang beautifully, but she also spoke out against the injustice of racism, regardless of how it affected her career.

It is equally important for us women to ask ourselves, "What do I want from my life?" We all struggle to answer this deceptively simple question. It takes courage to answer it honestly, but it takes far more courage to answer the question and then *act* on that answer. For example, Agnes de Mille realized she had "nothing to lose by being direct." She stuck to her vision for *Rodeo,* insisted on the set and composer she envisioned, and eventually produced her ballet—the way she wanted to. She believed in her vision, and the result was a great success. Dorothea Lange, having decided she wanted to become a photographer, asked for photography jobs, even though she had no experience and it was a profession that few women pursued.

In our society, we expect that all people should be treated with respect and dignity, but this has not always been true. Nina Simone faced discrimination and overcame social norms that promoted racial injustice. She confronted prejudice and disrespect directly, sometimes refusing to perform when an audience was unruly or rude. One evening, when she was only eleven years old, she even delayed her performance until her own parents were allowed to sit in the front row—seats that they had been asked to vacate for white people. Her demand for respect took courage.

Women's equality not only benefits women, but also brings a unique perspective to the world. For example, the brilliance of Dorothea Lange's photography was in large part due to her empathy for her subjects. She knew that to tell their story, she needed to earn their trust and to truly understand their lives.

Each of these women used her art to promote social justice. Coco Chanel used her designs to make women's lives easier and more comfortable, while Nina Simone was as committed to civil rights as she was to her music. Dorothea Lange's photographs convinced Washington of the need to establish sanitary camps for migrant families, and Virginia Woolf's writing pushed the question of equal rights for women.

Because the women in these books, and so many others like them, took risks and challenged society, women today have more opportunity than ever before. We have access to equal education, and we are making great strides in the workplace and in government.

As only the second woman from Minnesota ever elected to serve in Congress, I know how important it is to have strong female role models. My grandmothers were born in a time when women did not have the right to vote, but their granddaughter is now a Member of Congress. Their strength, wisdom, and courage inspire me. Other great women, such as Congresswoman Barbara Jordan and Congresswoman Shirley Chisholm, also inspired me with their leadership and determination to overcome gender and racial discrimination to serve in Congress with distinction.

Dorothea Lange once said, "I have learned from everything, and I'm constantly learning." I know that I too am constantly learning. I hope the women in this series will inspire you to learn and to lead with courage and determination. Art, as a profession or a hobby, can be either an expression or an agent of change. We need to continue to encourage women to add their voices to our society through art.

The women profiled in this series broke barriers, followed their hearts, refused to be intimidated, and changed our world. Their lives and successes should be a lesson to women everywhere. In addition, and importantly, they created lasting and meaningful art. I hope that you will enjoy this series as much as I have.

Nina at Carnegie Hall

Was she really a jazz singer? Was she more soul singer, blues singer or pop troubadour? She was all that and then some. Her craft ranged all over the black music map and beyond; she even found a home in Broadway songs. As Duke Ellington was fond of saying about artists he appreciated, she was "beyond category."
> —Willard Jenkins of Africana.com, April 22, 2003

Nina Simone's voice was unmistakable, moving from a seductive croon to a harsh growl, able to send shivers down your spine.
> —Emma Griffiths of Australian Broadcasting

When Nina Simone stepped onto the stage of New York City's Carnegie Hall on June 28, 2001, the audience sprang to its feet, erupting into raucous, wild applause. Fans ran up to the stage, crying out praise and showering the singer with flowers. Sixty-nine years old, wearing a floor-length gown of sparkling white,

Simone at Carnegie Hall, 2001. **At the time of this concert, Simone had been performing for almost half a century. She had progressed from a shy but gifted child to a music teacher, a lounge singer, a featured performer, an activist for civil rights, and an acknowledged queen of the American music industry. Her career had been influenced by the great anger she felt about the state of race relations in the United States, though, and she had developed a reputation as a "difficult" performer.**

the eccentric and much-loved diva had to be assisted onto the stage. Yet she was the most anticipated act in the 2001 JVC Jazz Festival.

At the conclusion of Simone's brief but characteristically mesmerizing performance, a woman leaving the festival remarked, "Well, she certainly can still command an audience." (*The New York Times,* July 2, 2001) Indeed, the woman known as the High Priestess of Soul had long ago established her reputation as a compelling and powerful live performer who held her audience enthralled.

After opening with her beloved classic "My Baby Just Cares for Me," Simone dedicated her program to "my ancestors Marcus Garvey, Langston Hughes, Lorraine Hansberry, Stokely Carmichael, and Paul Robeson." Throughout the show, her adoring public screamed, "We love you, Nina!" She responded, "I love you, too, sugar." When they yelled out their requests all at the same time, though, she reprimanded them: "I can't understand all of you at once. Say it again, but only one at a time."

And Simone couldn't help adding her thoughts about contemporary American politics when she performed "Why? (The King of Love Is Dead)," her own moving tribute to the assassinated civil rights leader Martin Luther King, Jr. According to a July 5, 2001, review in the New York *Amsterdam News*, Simone added the following:

It's a goddamn shame Martin Luther King is dead.
We're heading for the break with Bush in the White House.
That man has got to go.

When she'd finished a stirring rendition of another of her own songs, the movingly funky "Four Women," Simone departed the stage to applause and foot stomping that raged on for about twelve minutes, after which the *grande dame* returned and sang a quick reprise of the opening number.

She left the stage again, and the applause lasted another quarter of an hour. When she returned a second time, she proclaimed in signature Simone style, "I have no more to give you people; go the hell home." Her obedient congregation reluctantly but instantly obeyed.

Nina Simone: classically trained pianist, uncannily skilled improviser, elegant entertainer, gifted interpreter of others' songs, talented songwriter, outspoken militant, bitter expatriate, always a controversial figure. Like the woman herself, her music cannot be categorized easily: The Simone sound fused elements of classical, pop, jazz, gospel, folk, rhythm and blues, and soul. Vocally, she was incomparable. "Simone's moody-yet-elegant vocals are like no one else's, presenting a fiercely independent soul who harbors enormous (if somewhat hard-bitten) tenderness," writes music critic Richie Unterberger. (Erlewhine, 1020) Her live performances were legendary for their passion and immediacy. John S. Wilson of *The New York Times* wrote of her live version of the song "Everything Must Change" that "[i]t grew in the classic Simone manner from a mumble and a quaver through an intense, breathy declaration, swelling to a shout that burst into gospel excitement that swept the audience into the performance." (Brennan, 228)

Her intense commitment to her music was matched only by a fierce dedication to social justice. In the mid-1960s, Simone, then a young African-American woman from North Carolina, was among the first popular performers to sing about racism. She regularly appeared at civil rights fundraising events and marches, and she openly supported the Freedom Fighters and other activists on the front lines. One of her original songs, "Mississippi Goddam," became an anthem for the civil rights movement. But as she grew more militant in the late 1960s and the 1970s and became involved with radical groups such as the Black Panthers, her controversial politics threatened to overshadow her gifts as a musician and entertainer. The songs she wrote became angry and impassioned, and she spoke bluntly about her uncompromising views on racial equality. Nina Simone did not hesitate to voice her opinions, regardless of the effect they might have on her career. Analyst Brian Ward remembers the influence she had on the movement: "There was a self-possessed assurance—critics would call it arrogance and bloody-mindedness—about Simone; an independence of mind, spirit and action which seemed both refreshing and inspirational. It was this combination of message, music and manner which made her such a potent figure for the movement." (Ward, 301)

THE EXPERIENCE OF A NINA SIMONE CONCERT

From a review by *The Guardian*'s John Fordham of Simone's concert of December 14, 1997, given at the Barbican Centre in London:

From the moment the great soul-jazz diva came on stage, it was as if the countdown had been started on a fireworks extravaganza, but one designed by an artist with a loose wire or two. For with Nina Simone you never know just how much of the show is going to go off, or when—or even whether it will go off at all. There's an air of fearful expectation accompanying Simone's performances which compounds the already formidable effect of her whiplash tones, her alternately drumlike and elegiac piano-playing, her baleful stares and her bruised and brooding stage presence. When she was regularly appearing at Ronnie Scott's during the 1980s, her shows were among some of the most unforgettable public performances of recent times. . . .

In the 1970s, as her disillusionment with American racial attitudes intensified, so did her disgust with the entertainment industry. She abandoned the music business (temporarily) and went into self-imposed exile from her country of birth, living in Barbados, Liberia, Switzerland, and Holland before finally settling in the south of France. But her recordings continued to attract legions of fans, people who were captivated by her singular approach to music and her amazing ability to transform a song into an almost religious experience.

Over the years, Simone gradually returned to recording and giving performances, and her career experienced a resurgence

[A]n introduction . . . meticulously listed her considerable honorary titles and brought the house to its feet before she had even been guided to the piano stool. An aside to her band, a few hesitant steps towards the footlights, the merest shadow of a smile, and the roof almost fell in. . . .

She spat out "My Way" with a new ferocity, and "Pirate Jenny," one of her most spine-tingling interpretations, was delivered with an edge that rolled back the years. The audience went ballistic, the more so for the artist's stately progression to the front of the stage, head slowly panning around the auditorium, smile slowly spreading in what was clearly something near elation.

"Since you're all standing," she said, "I'd like you to join me in singing 'We Shall Overcome.'" We did. . . .

The High Priestess of Soul. Simone's involvement with the civil rights movement came to characterize her work almost as much as her melancholy songs of disappointed love. The depth of her commitment led fans to dub her "The High Priestess of Soul"—a name with which she was never comfortable. Simone resisted labels throughout her career.

in the late 1980s and the 1990s. By the turn of the millennium, with a new generation of fans, Simone's music had become more popular than ever. Her records, old and new, were selling well, and tracks from her albums were being traded through peer-to-peer file-sharing networks. Her songs have been featured on several film soundtracks and in commercials in the United States and abroad.

Nina Simone also performed for American audiences, offering, of course, her uncensored take on American politics and anything else that concerned her. Until the day of her death in 2003, Simone remained outspoken, indignant, and controversial. And, as her last concerts proved, the High Priestess of Soul certainly could always command an audience.

The Prodigy

1933–1944

I was born a child prodigy, darling. I was born a genius. Which means that at six months old my mum said that I knew what notes were.

— Nina Simone (quoted in Griffiths)

[E]xcellence is the best deterrent to racism or sexism.

— Oprah Winfrey (quoted in Lasker)

Eunice Kathleen Waymon (later called Nina Simone) was born on February 21, 1933, in a small town in North Carolina called Tryon. Eunice's parents, John Divine (named after St. John the Divine) and Mary Kate, already had five children when Eunice was born, and two more young Waymons arrived after her.

The Waymons hadn't always resided in Tryon. Eunice's great-great-grandmother, an American Indian, had lived just over the border in South Carolina, in plantation-heavy

A musical prodigy. Even at a very young age, Simone's gift for music was clear. She could sing and clap along with music even before she could speak, and she soon began to play familiar hymns on the piano by ear, without training of any kind. Her early exposure to musicianship fostered her skill at classical piano, and at this point, she did not think of herself as a singer.

Chesney County. She had married an African slave, and they had had a child together, a girl, born into slavery. Then their daughter had married another slave and given birth to Eunice's grandfather; he, in turn, had united with her grandmother, a light-complexioned woman of mixed lineage. In her autobiography, *I Put a Spell on You,* Nina Simone later wrote that her "[grandmother's] mother was half-Irish, the result of a plantation relationship my family has never been too interested in exploring." (1) Eunice's mother, Mary Kate, was their child, born November 20, 1902. Simone wrote in her autobiography that "[t]he blood in her veins is a rich mixture, drawn from white slave-owners, black slaves and the Indian people who were destroyed to make way for the plantations and the railroad." (2) Mary Kate met John Divine Waymon (born in 1899), an entertainer who danced, sang, and played the harmonica, in 1917. The two were married in 1922 and settled around Inman, South Carolina. Mary Kate gave birth to John Irvine in the following year. Lucille was born in 1924, followed by twin brothers Carroll and Harold in 1925. (Harold contracted spinal meningitis, which left him paralyzed on one side, at six weeks of age.)

While Mary Kate tended to the young family and household, John worked for a dry-cleaning business, though he was also a trained barber. Simone noted that "whatever job he was doing, he took the time to learn all about it; when he knew the details of his jobs he'd set about watching the people working around him and pretty soon he'd know their jobs too. . . . He turned his hand to anything." (*I Put a Spell on You,* 3) But John wanted to have his own business, to be his own boss. So when he found out that a town in the North Carolina mountains, Tryon, was looking for a barber, he jumped at the chance to apply. The Waymon family moved early in 1929, just a few weeks before the birth of Eunice's sister Dorothy on March 7.

LIFE IN TRYON

The Waymons were happy in Tryon. John's barbershop was doing well, but he also ran a dry-cleaning business and a truck driving operation to shelter and feed his large family.

Tryon's pleasant mountain climate—mild winters and cool summers—made it an appealing vacation spot for Southerners looking to escape the oppressive summer heat, and many of John's dry-cleaning customers were visitors to the town. Simone wrote that by 1930, "[m]y father was a respected member of the town's business community, Momma had made a good home and my brothers and sisters had settled in school and were doing well." (*I Put a Spell on You*, 5)

But then the Great Depression, which had begun in October 1929, reached Tryon, and the town gradually lost its summer visitors. Shops and business began to close permanently. By 1931, John Waymon had to shut down his dry-cleaning operations, and his truck driving jobs dwindled to a scant few. At Christmas of that year, he was forced to close his barbershop. In 1932, he finally found some work— the National Relief Agency needed truck drivers to distribute

THE GREAT DEPRESSION

On October 29, 1929, the American stock market crashed, igniting the economic blaze that led to the Great Depression. Banks closed, businesses failed, and by the time the Depression was over, about a decade later, more than 16 million people had lost their jobs. Although the entire country was affected by the Great Depression, the rural areas were particularly devastated. Farmers could no longer afford seeds, machinery, and land, so they took out loans; when they couldn't make payments on those loans, they went bankrupt. Still, African Americans in the South were hit the hardest; most of them worked as farm laborers, so when farmers started losing money, the laborers lost their jobs. To make matters worse, white people eventually started to take the jobs formerly held by black people.

provisions to the poor. So John earned a steady wage again, and he and his fellow truck drivers developed a system of trading food. Mary Kate and John, Simone wrote, were very proud of their garden. "Daddy would take whatever we had left over, like collard greens, string beans, tomatoes and sometimes eggs, to swap with people who had more sugar or flour, say, than they needed." (*I Put a Spell on You*, 6)

It was into this world that Eunice Kathleen Waymon was born in February 1933. Soon after her birth, John went off the NRA program. Visitors were slowly returning to Tryon, and some hotels had reopened for business, so John secured a job as a cook.

FAMILY AND VINEGAR PIE

"Most of what I remember from the very earliest part of my life is tied up with food and music," Simone wrote in her autobiography. She vividly remembered her mother's vinegar pie, dumplings, biscuits, brown betty, and lots of beans. Their small garden had grown into a little farm, with a cow, chickens, and pigs, plus produce. Although the Waymons were struggling like many other Depression-era families, Simone wrote, "I can't remember ever going hungry, not once. Momma made sure of that." (*I Put a Spell on You*, 7)

In 1935, the family had to move—John had stopped working, and they couldn't afford to stay in the bigger house. Then their second house was destroyed by fire, and they had to move again. Things took a turn for the worse when John was rushed to the hospital: He had a serious intestinal problem and needed surgery. He spent a few difficult weeks in the hospital, when the family didn't even know if he would survive; but at last he came home to recover.

With her mother now supporting the family as a housekeeper for a white family, and her siblings all in school, young Eunice, barely four years old, was left to take care of her father. While John lay outside, Eunice bathed him several times a day.

The two spent whole days together, and his health gradually improved. Together they planted and weeded the garden, and they played, too. "It was accepted by all my brothers and sisters that I was Daddy's favorite; he'd come right out and say so if anybody asked. . . . We came out of his sickness buddies, inseparable. . . . For the rest of my childhood I relied on him more than anyone else in the world, and he never let me down." (*I Put a Spell on You,* 11–12)

RELIGION AND MUSIC

Mary Kate was an elder at the Methodist church, and John was a deacon, so the Waymon children grew up in a very religious household in which liquor and profanity weren't allowed. But the Waymons raised their children in an environment infused with music. "Everything that happened to me as a child involved music," Simone later recalled. "It was part of everyday life, as automatic as breathing. . . . Everybody played music. There was never any formal training; we learned to play the same way we learned to walk, it was that natural." (*I Put a Spell on You,* 14) Mary Kate played the piano and constantly sang hymns around the house. John played piano, guitar, and harmonica. All the kids sang in the church choir and glee clubs and at social events.

When Eunice was born, the family had a pedal organ in the house. All the kids would fight over who would get to play first. But while the other Waymon children had a love of and skill with music, it soon became evident that it was Eunice who had a truly special gift. As a baby, she'd clap in time to the hymns. When the Waymons acquired a piano, Eunice, just three years old, taught herself to play some of her mother's favorite hymns by ear. Simone later wrote, "The whole family was astonished. Baby Eunice, whom they had never even seen sit at the organ before, was now playing hymns straight through without a mistake. Daddy just smiled and shook his head. To Momma's mind there

Simone's musical heritage. Simone was raised in a religious tradition that emphasized the vibrancy and the joy of music. Simone's mother was a minister, and all the Waymon children sang in the church choir and played or sang hymns around the house. To Simone, making music was "as natural as breathing." She included spirituals and gospel tunes in her repertoire throughout her career.

was only one explanation: I had received a gift from God." (*I Put a Spell on You*, 15)

By this time, Mary Kate had become an ordained Methodist minister and was preaching in churches around Tryon. When Eunice was just three and a half years old, she played the opening hymn at those services. By the time she was six years old, she had become the regular piano accompanist at her church. The churchgoers prayed, testified, shouted, and sang exuberantly, and Eunice accompanied them with rousing music. (She would continue to play at these services until she was twelve years old.) She and her sisters often sang spirituals together in their local church services, too. Many people felt that Eunice was a prodigy.

At home, her mother—who, Simone wrote, "was a fanatic [as far as church was concerned]"—forbade her from playing any music that wasn't religious. But her father would play or sing some of those banned songs while minister Mary Kate was out. Simone wrote, "in those days music involved no effort; the piano was a wonderful toy that I could play for hours without getting tired and although Momma tried to push my music down one particular road I had no preference for any individual style. In fact I liked to play as many different styles as possible, though I had to keep an eye out for Momma if I started wandering off the heavenly track." (*I Put a Spell on You*, 17)

But Eunice was learning much from the religious services. Her exposure to and participation in gospel music was profoundly shaping her rhythmic and improvisational abilities. "Someone would start off a song and I'd pick it up and keep playing. The person that had started it off might start to come through themselves so my job was to keep that rhythm repeating, building on it, keeping the feeling going. . . . Gospel taught me about improvisation, how to shape music in response to an audience and then how to shape the mood of the audience in response to my music. . . ." (*I Put a Spell on You*, 18–19)

PIANO LESSONS

When Eunice was about six years old, her father was still not well enough to hold a regular job, although he worked on and off as a gardener and handyman. Her mother was employed as a housekeeper for a white family, the Millers. Eunice's brother John Irvine and sister Lucille both worked and brought in money to help the family. Eunice, meanwhile, was beginning school. She attended Tryon's black junior school of about 150 students. (She, like the rest of her siblings, performed very well in school, usually taking home perfect grades.)

By this time, Mary Kate had started to spend a lot of time away from home, either attending church conventions or preaching at revivals throughout the county. Lucille assumed

Mary Kate's responsibilities during this period, running the household and taking care of the children. Eunice learned a lot from her older sister, and she grew to admire and respect her. She wrote, "I couldn't have had a more sensitive sister and she helped me get through what hurt most: I missed Momma all the time." (*I Put a Spell on You*, 21)

The most time Eunice spent with mother was at Mrs. Miller's house. She'd wait in the Miller kitchen while her mother finished her work. One day, Mrs. Miller—whom Simone later called "about the first white person I knew at all, to speak to"—visited the Waymons' church to hear Eunice play. She was so impressed with the young girl's ability that, after she found out from Mary Kate that the family couldn't afford piano lessons, she offered to pay for her lessons for a year. And, Simone wrote, when that year was over, "if I showed promise, then a way would be found to ensure they continued." (*I Put a Spell on You*, 21)

Eunice started studying with Muriel Massinovitch, an Englishwoman who had moved to Tryon with her husband, a painter. Mrs. Massinovitch, or "Mis Mazzy," as Eunice called her, was a petite, elegant woman. Simone remembered her as "very disciplined in the way she taught, very strict," though always polite. She loved the music of Johann Sebastian Bach and passed on her reverence for him to her young student. Indeed, she emphasized Bach over all other composers.

As Simone later recalled in her autobiography, she soon came to understand why Mis Mazzy permitted her to practice only Bach: "He is technically perfect. When you play Bach's music, you have to understand that he's a mathematician and all the notes you play add up to something—they make sense. They always add up to climaxes, like ocean waves getting bigger and bigger until after a while when so many waves have gathered you have a great storm. . . . Once I understood Bach's music, I never wanted to be anything other than a concert

Giving up seats. At a recital given when she was only eleven years old, Eunice Waymon protested her family's losing their front-row seats to a white family. Her stand recalls that of a key figure in the civil rights movement: Rosa Parks (shown here). A decade later, Parks started a revolution by refusing to give up her seat to a white man on a public bus in Montgomery, Alabama. Parks was arrested on December 1, 1955.

pianist; Bach made me dedicate my life to music, and it was Mrs. Massinovitch who introduced me to his world." (*I Put a Spell on You*, 23)

Mis Mazzy was affectionate to Eunice, and the two became friends. She was very aware of Eunice's prodigious musical gifts. After a year, Mis Mazzy took the funding of Eunice's lessons into her own hands by starting "The Eunice Waymon Fund." She wrote to local papers asking for donations, and she enlisted the assistance of her friends. Local churches took up a collection for the fund at services. This money paid for Eunice's lessons each week; the rest of it was saved for the future.

Eunice started to give regular recitals when she was about eight years old. She became famous around town. "White folks would point to me on the street and call me 'Mrs. Massinovitch's little coloured girl.' And so I was, although I didn't like the way they said it." (*I Put a Spell on You*, 24) Simone recalled later, in an interview with jazz critic John S. Wilson, that she was "the most outstandingly talented little girl in town, and . . . was colored." (Wilson 1960)

Eunice had been playing in front of people for years, but playing in front of *white* people threw her off balance. "I hated those recitals," she recalled. "Mis Mazzie never knew how tense I was and how scared those white people made me. I was split in half. . . . " (Wilson 1960) One recital in particular stood out. It happened when she was just around eleven years old, but it would serve as a point of reference throughout her life, a reminder about the importance of standing up for herself and protecting her dignity. She was seated at the piano, about to begin her performance at Tryon's town hall, when she noticed that her parents were being thrown out of their front-row seats—moved so a white family could sit there. Simone recalled, "Daddy and Momma were allowing themselves to be moved. Nobody else said anything, but I wasn't going to see them treated like that and stood up in my starched dress and said if anyone expected to hear me play then they'd better make sure that my family was sitting there in the front row where I could see them, and to hell with poise and elegance. So they moved them back. But my parents were embarrassed and I saw some of the white folks laughing at me." (*I Put a Spell on You*, 26) This moment represented a crossroads in Simone's life.

For the first time, she experienced directly and profoundly the sharp stab of racism.

Though Tryon was a typical Southern town at the time—schools, hotels, and public facilities were all segregated—relations between the black and white community always had been cordial. But as Eunice grew older, she began to wonder why she wasn't allowed to sit at the counter at the local pharmacy or use the restrooms at gas stations. The incident at the town hall made her keenly, painfully aware of racial prejudice. "All of a sudden it seemed a different world, and nothing was easy any more." (*I Put a Spell on You*, 26)

The Concert Pianist

1944–1954

I never thought about being black 'til I went up for a scholarship at the Curtis Institute.

—Nina Simone (quoted in Brennan)

By the time Eunice was finishing grade school, there had been some significant changes in the Waymon household. There were new additions to the family: Eunice's younger sister Frances was born in 1942, and her brother Sam in 1944. Her dear older sister Lucille had been married and moved out of the house, and Eunice would miss her terribly. Carroll was stationed in Virginia, and John Irvine was gone, too, though Eunice didn't really understand why. Simone later wrote, "To this day I don't know what passed between him and my father. . . . [Daddy] never talked about how he felt about losing his eldest son, which is what John Irvine's going

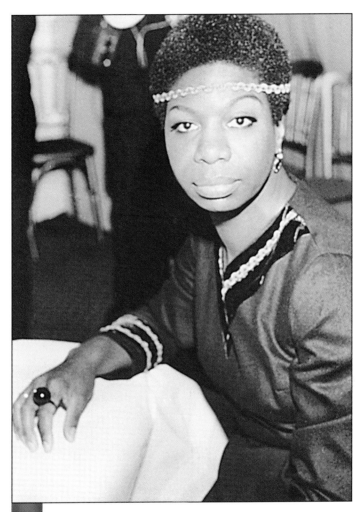

Before Nina Simone. During this period of her life, Eunice still thought of herself as a concert pianist, and she often had to sacrifice her social life for her studies. Through the Eunice Waymon Fund, assembled by her family and friends, she continued her piano lessons. When she graduated from high school, her work paid off: She had earned a scholarship to the prestigious Juilliard School of Music in New York City. This photograph was taken in London almost twenty years later, when her career as a singer was soaring.

amounted to. . . . Once he left I never saw him again for seventeen years." (*I Put a Spell on You*, 28)

The Waymons were now living in a house with running water, a wood stove, and three bedrooms. In 1943, Eunice's father had started working as a handyman. He took on many jobs, including gardening and waiting on tables, and he even opened up a store: He constructed an extension on their family house, from which he sold food, sandwiches, and candy.

Meanwhile, Eunice was undergoing some changes herself. She was just beginning to think "there was something wrong" with her. "I was already shy, and watching my friends get picked off one by one until I was left, alone, convinced me I was some kind of freak." (*I Put a Spell on You*, 31) Then she met someone who made an indelible impression on her life: Edney Whiteside.

He was Cherokee and had just moved into town with his family. "I wanted him from the moment I saw him," Simone later wrote. Both of them were shy, so they spent some time "darting glances when we each thought the other wasn't looking, neither saying a word." (*I Put a Spell on You*, 31) But one day, after church, Edney approached Eunice and asked if he could walk her home. The two of them started dating, and every Sunday they got together at four o'clock in the afternoon. The pair would drive to a nearby town to visit his grandmother and then sit and talk in his Chevy. Both families approved of their courtship.

Edney's companionship meant a lot to Eunice. Her dedication to music kept her from seeing friends often. She believed that her talent separated her from her family and friends, and she felt somewhat detached from her mother in particular. All those hours at the piano made her lonely, and she also felt tremendous pressure from all that was expected of her—by her parents, by her family, and by the community. Edney was a great comfort to her during those times, providing a respite and escape from her responsibilities.

HIGH SCHOOL

Meanwhile, the triumvirate of women in her life—her mother, Mrs. Miller, and Mis Mazzy—had decided that the next step for Eunice would be attendance at the Allen High School for Girls, paid for by the money from the Eunice Waymon Fund. A private boarding school located in nearby Asheville, Allen was "morally upright, had a good academic record. . . . [I]t was a protected environment, very protected" and seems to have been a relatively progressive school. "[B]lack pupils were accepted if they could pay the fees." (*I Put a Spell on You*, 32)

Eunice was very busy during her years at Allen High. She had lessons twice a week with Mrs. Joyce Carrol, a piano teacher whom Mis Mazzy respected. Of course, she sat at the piano and practiced daily, averaging about five hours a day. During this time, she learned more music of some of the masters, including Mozart, Beethoven, and Liszt, and she continued to play her dear Bach. She became a piano accompanist for the glee club and the school orchestra and at church. She also sang with the choir, played on the basketball team, acted in plays, and was president of the student council. Eunice enjoyed her classes and her teachers at Allen, and she performed with excellence, receiving perfect grades. She made some good friends at Allen High, too, with whom she played games, danced, and talked about boys and music.

Eunice and Edney wrote to each other every week. He visited her at school on Saturdays, and these visits were always chaperoned. When Edney's letters gradually tapered off, Eunice went home to see him one weekend. He told her he had started dating a friend of hers, Annie Mae. Simone wrote, "The way he put it was so simple, 'Yes, I'm going with her, you're not home. You're not home and I miss you too much.'" (*I Put a Spell on You*, 35)

When graduation time arrived, Eunice was the valedictorian

of her class. She also had qualified for a scholarship to the renowned Juilliard School of Music in New York City—a very rare opportunity for an African-American girl in the 1950s. Eunice was on her way to fulfilling her own dreams, as well as those of her mother and Mis Mazzy. It was their intention that Eunice Waymon become a concert pianist—the first African-American concert pianist.

Mary Kate and Mis Mazzy had a particular plan: Eunice would attend Juilliard and then take the scholarship examination for the prestigious Curtis Institute of Music in Philadelphia. Although Eunice had spent hours and hours of her life playing the piano, preparing to become a classical pianist, she was reluctant to leave Edney behind. Around this time, Simone wrote, "Edney said 'If you go to New York you won't ever come back, we both know that. So if we don't get married now it will never happen, and if you go I'll marry your best friend.'" It was a painful choice for Eunice. "On one side was music, Mis Mazzy, my family, all those long hours of practice and the aspirations of the town I was born in and of my race as well, of my own people. On the other side was Edney, all alone."(*I Put a Spell on You*, 36)

Eunice felt torn, but she ultimately decided to follow her career dreams and go to New York. This was excruciatingly difficult for her. She later wrote, "I knew how lonely music made me, how I couldn't talk about it to anyone and how the hours I devoted to it stopped me from having a normal life. . . . In Edney, whom I loved and who loved me, I had someone to connect with, to tie me to the real world, to love more than music."(*I Put a Spell on You*, 35)

JUILLIARD

New York City was an entirely different world from the one she had been accustomed to. She lived uptown on 145th Street in Harlem, with a preacher friend of her mother's, Mrs. Steinermayer. At first, the shy country girl was intimidated and shocked by much about New York, including the men who constantly drank and cursed loudly on the corner, but she gradually explored her new city. "I was so shy that making new friends was impossible. . . . I walked around the two or three blocks by my house just looking around, never daring to open my mouth." (*I Put a Spell on You*, 39) It was a drastic change from the small-town life of Tryon.

Eunice attended her classes at Juilliard every day, and she practiced at the school daily, too. She studied under Dr. Carl Friedberg, a pianist and instructor of considerable renown. He had studied under Clara Schumann, one of the most accomplished pianists and composers of the nineteenth century, and he had gone on to teach many widely acclaimed students of his own. "A great teacher," Simone recalled, "very gifted. . . . [H]e was the greatest musician I had met up to that time and I learned something new each time I sat down to play for him. . . . I was the only black student he had, but nobody made any mention of it and the fact was of no interest to me." (*I Put a Spell on You*, 39)

Eunice was wholly committed to classical piano, and she felt that she truly had found her calling. "Studying under Dr. Friedberg gave me a satisfaction and happiness I couldn't explain, but I knew this was what I was born to do, what all those hours of practice had been about, and it was leading to my destiny, the classical concert stage." (*I Put a Spell on You*, 40)

Adhering to the original plan, Eunice was determined to win the scholarship to the Curtis Institute. She prepared wholeheartedly for the exam with Dr. Friedberg. She also visited Mis Mazzy and Mrs. Carrol, who listened to Eunice's playing and offered their guidance. She needed that scholarship. Even though she was on scholarship at Juilliard, she still had to dip into the fund and use $25 a week for lessons. There

Carl Friedberg. **At Juilliard, Eunice studied with Dr. Friedberg, one of the most renowned pianists of the time and a student of the great Clara Schumann. She was his only African-American student, but, unlike in Tryon, at Juilliard this meant very little. Friedberg's mentoring led Eunice to pursue classical piano with passion and to prepare wholeheartedly for the scholarship examination for the Curtis Institute of Music.**

wasn't much left in the fund, but Eunice felt ready to tackle the exam and do well.

The whole family was thrilled about Eunice's move to Philadelphia. After he had completed his army service,

Carroll decided to live in the City of Brotherly Love, where opportunities were much better. And Lucille was living there, too, with her husband. With Eunice now heading to Curtis, Mary Kate and John decided that it was an appropriate time to leave Tryon, so the whole family moved to Philadelphia. (Mary Kate, Frances, and Sam moved up in September 1950, but John stayed down in Tryon for a while to put things in order.)

Eunice took the examination for Curtis late in the year, then returned to New York to study with Dr. Friedberg for as long as she could. Then she heard from the Curtis Institute. It wasn't the news that she and her family had anticipated and planned for. Eunice was rejected, and the news destroyed her. She later wrote in her autobiography, "When I was rejected by the Curtis Institute it was as if all the promises ever made to me by God, my family and my community were broken and I had been lied to all my life." (*I Put a Spell on You*, 41) She had worked so hard, sacrificed so much of her life to achieve her goal of becoming a concert pianist, never once even considering the possibility that her ambitions wouldn't come to fruition. She'd never imagined that she might not be good enough. She would be haunted by that rejection for the rest of her life. Many years after the disappointing incident, in January 1997, Simone said in an interview for *Details*, "I started off very pure and innocent and I believed till the last minute that I'd be that concert pianist. It still takes a long time for me to accept the fact that it's never going to happen the way I dreamed it." (Bardin)

Still, when her brother Carroll shared with her something that he had heard, Eunice started to think there might have been other reasons why she was not admitted. She later wrote, "The story that Carroll heard through my uncle and his friends, black and white, was that the Institute wanted to enroll black students, but if blacks were going to be admitted then they were not going to accept an unknown

BLACK PERFORMERS AND DISCRIMINATION

African-American musicians, dancers, singers, and other artists who performed in the United States, regardless of their stature or popularity, had to contend with discrimination before the civil rights movement. When jazz pianist and composer Eubie Blake was at the height of his career (in the 1930s), he had to send home his clothes to be washed because laundry businesses refused to handle the clothing of black people. Touring performers had to make special arrangements to stay with friends or at shady boardinghouses, because hotels wouldn't allow African Americans to sleep there. Bandleader Cab Calloway tried to protect his musicians from prejudice in the 1930s and 1940s, renting out entire sleeping cars for them, but he couldn't shelter them from other abuse. A Mississippi police officer held a gun to the head of one of Calloway's band members when he didn't call the officer "sir." Calloway eventually stopped touring the South because he feared for the safety of his musicians.

Marian Anderson, regarded as the world's greatest contralto of her time, wasn't exempt from racial prejudice, either. She often was refused service at concert halls, restaurants, and hotels. In 1939, the Daughters of the American Revolution (DAR) prevented the singer from appearing at Constitution Hall in Washington, D.C. But, in response to massive protests supporting Anderson, the Department of the Interior, with the support of First Lady Eleanor Roosevelt, scheduled Anderson to give a performance on the steps of the Lincoln Memorial on Easter Sunday. Anderson, with 75,000 people in attendance and millions of radio listeners, gave one of her most memorable concerts. Simone called Anderson "one of the great heroes of my family." (*I Put a Spell on You*, 42)

Marian Anderson at the Lincoln Memorial. Eunice Waymon's rejection from the Curtis Institute changed the course of her life—and twentieth-century music—forever. She believed it was due to racism, as the social tide of the time was against black performers. Singer Marian Anderson faced racism head-on in 1939: After a conservative group denied her permission to perform in Washington's Constitution Hall, she held an open-air concert on the steps of the Lincoln Memorial. Thousands of people attended, including cabinet secretaries and a justice of the Supreme Court, and millions more listened. It was an early and crucial step in the civil rights movement.

black, that if they were going to accept an unknown black then it was not going to be an unknown black girl, and if they were going to admit an unknown black girl it wasn't going to be a very poor unknown black girl." (*I Put a Spell on You*, 42) Many people, both white and black, told her that she was denied entry to Curtis because she was black. A lot of thoughts were running through her head at the time— shame, anger, disbelief—so she wasn't sure what to believe.

But, she wrote, "One thing was for sure: I was finished with music." (*I Put a Spell on You*, 43)

Eunice came to fervently believe that racism was the reason she was refused entry to Curtis. In a 1985 statement, she said, "I never thought about being black 'til I went up for a scholarship at the Curtis Institute. . . . I was too good not to get it, but they turned me down. . . . I couldn't get over it [then], I haven't gotten over it now." (Brennan, 229)

IN PHILADELPHIA

Eunice's money from the fund had almost run out, so she decided to stay in Philadelphia with her family. She was so dejected about the rejection from Curtis that she took a job as a photographer's assistant. She felt saddened and resentful, but, after much encouragement and persuasion from her brother Carroll, she decided not to give up and to use the little money left in the fund to pay for her own private lessons.

Eunice began studying with Vladimir Sokhaloff at Curtis, and gradually she regained her confidence and pride. She then rethought her plans for the future and made the decision to do whatever she could to continue studying classical piano. She took a job as an accompanist for vocal students at the Arlene Smith Studio, where she expanded her repertoire to include popular songs and old standards. She worked eight-hour days five days a week, earning $50 weekly. She used half of her earnings to keep up her studies with Sokhaloff, and soon she started offering lessons to students of her own.

All this was happening between about 1952 and 1954. Eunice had her own apartment (a storefront, the same space in which she gave her piano lessons), a dog named Sheba, and one good friend. But when she found out that one of her students—one of her least talented ones, at that—was going to spend the summer working in Atlantic City, New Jersey, playing piano at a bar and making twice as much money as Eunice made, Eunice decided to do the same.

Eunice managed to secure a gig playing at a place called the Midtown Bar and Grill, located about two blocks from the famous Atlantic City boardwalk. Though it was a seedy Irish bar with sawdust on the floor, it was to become the launching pad for Nina Simone's career in show business.

The Chanteuse

1954–1959

Soulful, juicy, big, fat, round, mellifluous—shall I go on?
— Jazz pianist Joe Chindamo,
on Simone's voice (quoted in Griffiths)

Atlantic City's Midtown Bar and Grill, situated on Pacific Avenue near the boardwalk by the sea, seems an unlikely venue from which to launch a career in show business. But that's exactly what the small, dingy Irish bar became for Eunice Waymon. She took the job at the Midtown simply to make money so she could continue her studies in classical piano. She never imagined for a moment that she was on her way to becoming an internationally known popular performer.

Before she left for Atlantic City in the summer of 1954, she worried about her mother's reaction to the news that she would be playing piano in a bar. In her mother's mind, working in a

Atlantic City. Turned down by the Curtis Institute, Eunice Waymon began to accept students of her own. Before long, though, she realized that her students were making far more for performances in Atlantic City than she was making for teaching them. In 1954, Eunice braved the objections of her mother and accepted a job with the Midtown Bar and Grill. It was at the Midtown that "Nina Simone" was born, and the gig at the Grill began to establish Simone as a musical force to be reckoned with.

bar was sinful, no "different from working in the fires of hell," Simone later wrote. (*I Put a Spell on You*, 49) Eunice wanted to take whatever steps she could to prevent her mother from finding out. She didn't want to embarrass her mother and the rest of her family, so she decided to assume a stage name. She had liked it when an old Hispanic boyfriend, Chico, called her "Nina"—*niña* being Spanish for "little girl." And she had always loved the name "Simone," ever since she had first watched Simone Signoret act in French films. It was in this way that Eunice Waymon became Nina Simone.

THE RISE OF THE DIVA

Nina Simone, the artist formerly known as Eunice Waymon, arrived in Atlantic City unsure of what to expect. She had never been inside a bar in all her life. But she was determined to present herself with dignity and pride, something she would continue to do throughout her career. She walked up to the bar in her long chiffon gown and asked to speak to the owner, Harry Steward; then she ordered a glass of milk, which prompted a few of the old Irish men sitting around the bar to laugh. Simone later wrote, "The Midtown was just one long room with the bar stretching two-thirds of the way down one wall. . . . There was a door by the end of the bar, and behind that was a room where they put the drunks to sleep it off when they'd had too much to make it home. Sawdust on the floor. A joint. No other word for it—at least no decent one." (*I Put a Spell on You*, 49)

Steward appeared and showed Simone the piano and the stool, which were directly under a leaky air conditioner. He then stuck an opened-up umbrella into the ceiling; this way, the water would dribble into a puddle on the floor by one of the tables instead of on top of the piano. He told Simone to come back in an hour to begin her show.

Simone returned and immediately set to work, playing as instructed from nine o'clock at night until four o'clock in the morning. (Every hour she had a fifteen-minute break, when she would sip her glass of milk at the bar.) She wrote about that first night, "I sat on stage a diva, a professional entertainer for the first time, and played to an audience of drunken Irish bums." She came to the bar equipped with an arsenal of hundreds of popular songs and numerous classical pieces, and blended all the different styles that she had been exposed to over the years. She wrote, "What I did was combine them: I arrived prepared with classical pieces, hymns, and gospel songs and improvised on those, occasionally slipping in a part from a popular tune. Each song—which isn't the right way to describe what I was playing—lasted anywhere between thirty and ninety minutes. I just sat down, closed my eyes, and drifted away on the music." (*I Put a Spell on You*, 50)

Simone was developing a signature style, one that was entirely different from anything else that was happening in music at the time. By now, she had become familiar with such song stylists as Billie Holiday, Hazel Scott, Louis Armstrong, Kitty White, and Sarah Vaughan. Her exposure to them surely informed her enticing new sound. She laced pop and jazz, along with gospel music, spirituals, and some folk, over a framework of classical music, and it resulted in an exciting and innovative musical fusion. Simone was showcasing her amazing gift for improvisation, a talent she had honed over the years since she played the piano for her mother's sermons.

Steward thought he had hired a singer, and at the end of her first night, after complimenting her performance, he asked why she hadn't sung. When Simone said, "I'm only a pianist," he replied, "Well, tomorrow night you're either a singer or you're out of a job." (*I Put a Spell on You*, 51) So, the next night, she began her illustrious career as a vocalist—and it all came about because of a misunderstanding. Despite the fact that she never had sung alone in front of an audience before, Nina Simone sang, in her own singular style. Steward was pleased, the crowd liked it, and even Simone was happy with it.

Prior to her gig at the Midtown, Simone had hated popular music. She'd much preferred playing the classical masters. She had associated popular songs with the unpleasant experience she'd had accompanying lackluster students at the Arlene Smith Studio. But when she mixed classical and popular pieces together in her Midtown performances, "I found a pleasure in it almost as deep as the pleasure I got from classical music. Playing at the Midtown made me looser and more relaxed about music. I was creating something new, something that came out of me. . . . I used my voice as a third layer, complementing the other two layers, my right and my left hands. When I got to the part where I used elements of popular songs

I would simply sing the lyric and play around with it, repeating single lines over again, repeating verses, changing the order of the words. . . ."(*I Put a Spell on You*, 51)

As she performed that summer, she noticed that the audience of "old drunks" was gradually being replaced by a younger group of customers. College students from around the Atlantic City area started to fill the Midtown, attracted by Simone's wholly new and vital musical sound. She was carving out a reputation for herself, and her live shows were winning her a loyal following.

ATLANTIC CITY

There was a long period of time, from the 1880s all the way up to the late 1940s, when Atlantic City, New Jersey, was a major vacation resort for Americans on the East Coast. The first amusement pier, featuring carnival rides and saltwater taffy shops, opened in 1882. Eventually, Atlantic City became famous for novelty acts, such as animal shows and bizarre, sideshow-like events, offered on its boardwalk. In the 1920s, flashy, exciting Atlantic City was considered *the* tryout town for theatrical productions headed for Broadway. By the 1930s, Atlantic City's nightlife scene boasted the biggest stars from the jazz world—especially at Club Harlem and other venues on Kentucky Avenue. It was a prestigious place, attracting big celebrities and wealthy Americans for the first half of the twentieth century. But after World War II, when air travel became more available, tourism to the town sharply declined. By the time Nina Simone started performing there, the city had lost much of its former luster. More people were flying to far-off destinations, like Florida and the Caribbean, so businesses closed and the town fell on hard times. It didn't regain popularity until the 1970s, when Atlantic City legalized gambling.

SUPPER CLUBS

When the summer was over, Simone returned to Philadelphia to resume teaching her private lessons and studying with Sokhaloff. But she began to rethink her plans for the future. Since she'd earned a lot more money through performing than through teaching, she felt that if she was even more successful as a performer, then she might soon be able to afford full-time study at a classical conservatory.

Simone's second summer in Atlantic City, the summer of 1955, was much more enjoyable than the first. She continued to pack in the Midtown Bar and Grill. Word had spread of her virtuosity at the piano, her distinctive vocal style, and her unique musical approach. And she had started to make some friends, many of whom admired her music. One of those friends was a man named Ted Axelrod. He was a huge fan of music in general, and he had a large record collection. One night, he lent her a Billie Holiday album and asked her if she would sing a track from it—a song called "I Loves You Porgy," from the 1934 George and Ira Gershwin opera *Porgy and Bess*. Simone performed the heartrending piece, everyone loved it, and it soon became an integral part of her repertoire.

She dreaded going back to teaching, and the enthusiastic response for her performances at the Midtown compelled her to try to land some similar work in Philadelphia. So she contacted the agent who had set up her gig in Atlantic City, and, soon enough, Simone was playing at dinner clubs in the Philadelphia area that were more "upscale." She first played at a local supper club, and then she moved on to other venues—places with names like the High-Thigh. Simone was broadening her audience and widening her appeal. But she found the clientele at these Philadelphia clubs much less attentive than the young customers in Atlantic City. They often viewed her music as part of the background to their dates, and they had a tendency to chatter while Simone played. But she had also had complaints with some of the Midtown crowd. If an inebriated customer

From pianist to singer. When she accepted the job at the Midtown, Simone still considered herself a pianist, albeit a frustrated one. After her first show, though, she was faced with a choice: to become a singer, too, or lose her job. So she sang, and soon she found real pleasure in mixing the classical and popular styles. This was the beginning of a six-decade performing career, and Simone was already winning devoted fans.

shouted while Simone was performing, she'd stop playing and wouldn't begin again until the drunk had been thrown out of the bar. "If an audience disrespects me it is insulting the music I play and I will not continue, because if they don't want to listen then I don't want to play. An audience chooses to come and see me perform; I don't choose the audience. I don't need them either, and if they don't like my attitude then they don't have to come and see me." (*I Put a Spell on You*, 52)

She maintained this position, often indignantly, throughout her performing career.

When Simone was entertaining in Philadelphia, she decided to tell her mother the truth about what she was doing. She told Mary Kate that she was playing at clubs and performing some popular music—what her mother considered "the devil's music"—so she could raise the funds to continue her classical education and follow her dream of becoming the first black classical pianist. It didn't matter; Mary Kate still disapproved. Meanwhile, Simone believed her father secretly was thrilled. Even so, he warned her about the temptations and dangers of the performing life, remembering his own experiences as an entertainer long ago.

In the summer of 1956, Simone became acquainted with Don Ross, a white man who had heard about her music through some of his friends. The two started talking at the Midtown, and he quickly became a regular at her shows. Simone wrote that "he thought of himself as a beatnik. . . . If you asked him what he did he'd say he was a painter or a drummer—depending on what kind of mood he was in—but in fact he was a pitchman and travelled up and down the East Coast working the fairs." (*I Put a Spell on You*, 56)

Ross and Simone would hang out together between sets, and he began to visit her during the day, introducing her to some of his friends. Simone and Ross eventually started dating, though half-heartedly on Simone's side. Simone later wrote, "If I didn't feel a great deal of passion for him it was nice to wake up in his arms rather than on my own in a cold room. . . . He loved me, and I needed to be loved." (*I Put a Spell on You*, 56)

That summer, Simone also met Jerry Fields, an agent from New York City who had taken an interest in her music. On the same night they were introduced, Simone later wrote, Fields promised to find her jobs in New York that would pay more money than she had been offered by anyone else. Fields went on to become Simone's sole agent for the next five years.

While Simone was back performing in Philadelphia that fall, Fields set up several shows for her in New York City, Upstate New York, and the popular off-Broadway town of New Hope, Pennsylvania. The gig at New Hope's Bucks County Playhouse Inn, brought on two unexpected and highly significant events: Simone met and played with another musician who was remarkably in sync with her, and she recorded the demo tape that would lead to her first record deal.

A NEW DIRECTION

At her gig at the Playhouse Inn, a guitarist named Al Schackman approached Simone and told her he'd heard some positive things about her and her music. Although initially Simone was less than enthusiastic, she allowed him to set up his equipment. When he was ready, she started playing her first song, the melancholy Rodgers and Hart tune "Little Girl Blue." (Simone was known for setting up counterpoints between her songs and classical or other well-known tunes; one example of this was her interpolation of the Christmas carol "Good King Wenceslas" in "Little Girl Blue.") The experience of performing with Schackman astonished her. She later wrote that, with Schackman, "I'd discovered the joy of sharing [the music]. . . . Al was right there with me from the first moment, as if we had been playing together all our lives. It was more than that even: it was as if we were one instrument split in two—I, the piano, Al, the guitar." They became fast friends, and Simone seemed to have found something of a soul mate in him. "Sometimes we'd be talking on the phone to each other and we'd say exactly the same word at exactly the same time." (*I Put a Spell on You*, 59) The two would remain great friends and musical colleagues for forty years.

After the New Hope show, Jerry Fields telephoned Simone to let her know that a demo she had made at the Inn had been heard by Sid Nathan. Nathan was the owner of a record label called Bethlehem Records, a sister company of King Records.

Billie Holiday in 1954. As Simone's original style became more popular, observers compared her to the other great singers of the time. Billie Holiday has always been one of the primary comparisons: Simone later sang a number of songs that Holiday had popularized, such as "Strange Fruit" and "I Loves You Porgy." There were also parallels with substance abuse and domestic violence, but the similarities end there. Simone herself never agreed with the comparison and always resented being categorized.

The following day, Nathan met with the songstress to discuss recording her album. He came armed with his own ideas about what Simone should include on the record and with whom she should perform. Simone wrote that when she declared she would make an album only if she could choose the songs and musicians herself, he "started gulping like a fish." Since her heart was still in classical piano, she really had no wish to become famous as a performer of popular music. But Nathan eventually agreed to let Simone record songs that she selected herself. After consulting with Fields about money, she decided to accept the deal.

5

The Star

1958–1962

On stage, her presence was magic. . . . She had such charisma. She almost didn't have to sing. The way she held herself, her energy, her majesty. She was a queen up there. Everyone felt it. Performing on stage, she forgot everything else. What a voice! I'd say at least three-quarters of her concerts were absolute triumphs.

> — Raymond Gonzalez (quoted in Zwerin)

I love them to love me and if they're going to have an idol, they should have a good one, and that's me.

> — Nina Simone (quoted in Griffiths)

Fourteen hours after Simone went into the studio, she completed the album called *Jazz as Played in an Exclusive Side Street*, also known as *Little Girl Blue*, recorded with Jimmy Bond on bass and Al Heath on drums. Her friend and associate Al Schackman was touring with Burt Bacharach at the

Nina triumphant. Simone had no desire to pursue a career as a popular singer, for her heart was still in her classical studies. But in the years following her recording debut, *Jazz as Played in an Exclusive Side Street* (*Little Girl Blue*), Simone became known for her Midtown style. Millions of her records sold, both legally and illegally recorded. Although she ran into a few obstacles with the seedier side of the recording industry, Simone came out on top. This photograph was taken at a concert in Paris in 1991.

time, so, much to Simone's regret, he was unable to make it to the session.

The songs captured that day were representative of a typical night at the Midtown, though the record was devoid of Simone's instrumental improvisations that live audiences received. Of course, Simone's signature version of "I Loves You Porgy" was included. The first track on the album was the classic "Mood Indigo," followed by "Don't Smoke in Bed." "He Needs Me," a song Simone picked up after hearing Peggy Lee's rendition, came next, followed by the title track, "Little Girl Blue." "Plain Gold Ring" followed, a piece Simone had learned from harpist Kitty White. Also contained on the album were an instrumental version of "You'll Never Walk Alone" (from the 1945 Rodgers and Hammerstein musical *Carousel*), another instrumental titled "Good Bait," and the Simone classics "Love Me or Leave Me" and "My Baby Just Cares for Me." (Simone claims that this last piece was included at the session because Nathan wanted an "up-tempo number" to finish the day.) When two of the scheduled songs were scrapped, Simone— though she had never written a song before—composed replacement songs on the spot: "Central Park Blues" (they had just been in the famed Manhattan park shooting publicity photos for the album) and "African Mailman." The latter ultimately didn't make it onto *Side Street*; but Bethlehem used it on a later album, along with two other tunes taped at this session ("For All We Know" and the traditional spiritual "He's Got the Whole World in His Hands").

At the end of the recording session, Simone was handed a piece of paper, which she unthinkingly signed. Unknowingly, she had, with a turn of her hand, relinquished all of her rights to the album. It was a mistake, she wrote in her autobiography, that would ultimately cost her over a million dollars. It was only the first in a long series of problematic dealings with the recording industry that Simone would experience over the course of her career.

Jazz as Played in an Exclusive Side Street/Little Girl Blue was released in mid-1958, marking Simone's debut as an official artist. But, as she later wrote in her autobiography, "The first album I ever made was a pirate that I never got paid for." (*I Put a Spell on You*, 57) During one of her gigs in Philadelphia, someone had illegally recorded her performance. The bootleg eventually appeared as an album called *Starring Nina Simone*. It contained such classic Simone gems as "I Loves You Porgy," "Baubles, Bangles, and Beads," "Since My Lover Has Gone," and the Norwegian traditional "Black Is the Color of My True Love's Hair," all performed in her distinctive vocal style. In 1965, she took the label to court to prevent the company from making any more money from the pirated album.

A STAR IS BORN

Nothing significant occurred with *Little Girl Blue* until a Philadelphia radio deejay named Sid Marx started playing "I Loves You Porgy" three or four times in a row. The station was soon bombarded with requests for the song, and "Porgy" became a hit in the city. Within a few weeks, radio listeners in New York fell for Simone's plaintive, yet understated, rendition of the Gershwin tune, and it played again and again across the airwaves up and down the East Coast. Soon it caught on across the country, and by the summer of 1959, it had climbed up the national pop charts into the top twenty. It also landed the number two spot on the R&B charts. "I Loves You Porgy" went on to sell a million copies. It was Simone's first major success, firmly establishing her reputation in the American cultural firmament. (Unbelievably, though, it was the only one of Simone's songs ever to make it to the U.S. top-twenty charts.)

In those first months after the album was released, while Simone's star was beginning to rise, she decided to marry Don Ross. It was to be a very short-lived marriage, dissolving in 1959 when she walked out on him. Simone wrote, "I realized marrying Don was a mistake before that first month ended. . . . I had originally married Don so I'd never be alone, but after we had got married I went home hoping he wouldn't be there." (*I Put a Spell on You*, 63) By then, she was living in New York, having been convinced by her agent Jerry Fields that she needed to be there instead of in Philadelphia if she wanted to succeed. Although she was tremendously busy performing, she still had difficulty making ends meet. She continued to send money home to her mother, and she paid for rent and food for Ross and herself. Because she needed still more to help pay the bills, she also worked as a maid for a white family. After all, her heart was still in classical music, and she was still intent on furthering her classical studies.

The unexpected success of "I Loves You Porgy" led to yet more bookings for Simone, and those bookings gradually became bigger and bigger. On September 12, 1959, Simone debuted at the famed Town Hall in New York City, where the groundbreaking African-American singer Marian Anderson had launched her operatic career in 1935. It was at this concert that Simone really became a known singer. She appeared with Horace Silver and J.J. Johnson, two well-established and widely respected musicians. In a review of the show for *The New York Times*, critic John S. Wilson wrote that Simone "easily held her own" in the company of Silver and Johnson. She was a commanding performer, and she captivated both audience and critics. Wilson called Simone "a gifted interpreter, a singer who makes each song her own." "By the time she has finished turning a song this way and that way," he wrote, "poking experimentally into unexpected crannies she finds in it, or suddenly leaping on it and whaling the daylights out of it, the song has lost most of its original colorization and has become, one might say, 'Simonized.'" (Wilson 1959)

Simone's stage presence was so compelling that she

developed an almost cult-like following among her fans, which continues to this day. She became known for her powerful live performances, and it was, in fact, the live recording of that Town Hall show that truly propelled her to stardom.

GEORGE GERSHWIN (1898–1937)

The masterful composer George Gershwin, the son of Russian-Jewish immigrants, began his legendary career in his teens by playing the piano in New York's famous Tin Pan Alley. He was soon being paid to write songs for Harms Music. His first hit was "Swanee," made famous by Al Jolson in 1919. Eventually, he was writing full-length musicals and operas. In the 1920s, his legendary partnership with his brother Ira (1896–1983), a lyricist, began. Together, they churned out standards such as "I've Got a Crush on You," "Embraceable You," "They Can't Take That Away From Me," "Someone to Watch Over Me," and "Our Love Is Here to Stay," songs originally included in scores for shows and Hollywood films. George Gershwin's music was a rhythmic synthesis of European and African-American styles. While he was penning this seemingly endless stream of catchy popular tunes, he was also composing more serious music, such as the tone poem "Rhapsody in Blue" and "An American in Paris." But the opera *Porgy and Bess*, written in 1935, is widely hailed as his masterpiece. Based on a novel about African-American life by DuBose Heyward, *Porgy and Bess* first opened to mixed reviews. But five years after George's sudden death, the work received the critical and popular success it was due. In addition to "I Loves You Porgy," it contains beloved songs such as "Summertime" and "I Got Plenty of Nuttin'." It has been called the first truly American opera.

The album, recorded in September and October 1959, was appropriately entitled *Nina Simone at Town Hall*. It featured two versions of "Summertime," another selection from the Gershwin opera *Porgy and Bess* that had been popularized by Billie Holiday. Other songs included were Holiday's "Fine and Mellow," "The Other Woman," Irving Berlin's "You Can Have Him (I Don't Want Him)," and an instrumental composed by Simone, "Under the Lowest," which revealed her genius on the piano. An especially breathtaking piece on this album is Simone's rendition of "Black Is the Color of My True Love's Hair." Upon first hearing this track, British music writer David Nathan wondered, "Who was this woman who could go from soprano tenderness to dark velvet in a millisecond?" (Nathan, 49) (Nathan later became the head of Simone's British fan club.)

In the liner notes to the live album *The Amazing Nina Simone*, Roger Caras writes, "Nina brings to each number a special quality that comes from brilliant musicianship with an almost philosophical understanding of the words. When Nina sings the word 'love,' it isn't a word combined from four letters out of the alphabet but an emotional experience you can feel." (Caras, 1)

IN A CATEGORY ALL HER OWN

By the time the Town Hall live album was released in early 1960, Simone had already switched from Bethlehem to the Colpix label, a division of Columbia Pictures. Joyce Selznick, the eastern talent scout for Columbia Pictures, had arranged an audition for Simone with Paul Wexler of Colpix. Simone hadn't been very pleased with Bethlehem's treatment of her or the promotion of *Little Girl Blue*. Since her agreement with Bethlehem was for only one album, Simone decided to sign with Colpix, which offered her a long-term contract.

The first album Simone completed with Colpix was *The Amazing Nina Simone*, which was also recorded in New York in

LANGSTON HUGHES
(1902–1967)

angston Hughes, born in Joplin, Mississippi, was a novelist, essayist, and dramatist, but he was best known for his output as a poet. Hughes was one of the finest and most versatile writers of the Harlem Renaissance, a period during the 1920s and 1930s in which African-American artists, dancers, and writers expressed themselves and celebrated the vitality and artistry of their culture. Called the "Poet Laureate of Harlem," he used black vernacular and the beat and rhythms of jazz and blues in his poetry to achieve a new poetic style. *The Weary Blues* (1926), his first collection of poems, established his reputation. Other poetic works include *Shakespeare in Harlem* (1942) and *Montage of a Dream Deferred* (1951). He also wrote the play *Mulatto* (1935) and the collection of short stories *The Ways of White Folks* (1934). In an essay that he wrote in 1926 for *The Nation*, he made a statement that became famous: "We younger Negro artists now intend to express our individual dark-skinned selves without fear or shame. If white people are pleased we are glad. If they aren't, it doesn't matter. We know we are beautiful. And ugly too. . . . If colored people are pleased we are glad. If they are not, their displeasure doesn't matter either. We build our temples for tomorrow, as strong as we know how and we stand on the top of the mountain, free within ourselves."

Hughes was ardently committed to celebrating blackness, and when he met Simone, he gave her books about black pride and history. She later wrote, "I'd go over to his place in Harlem and over dinner—southern style—we'd talk, recite songs and poems and drink wine until the sun came up." (*I Put a Spell on You*, 96)

1959. But before that album was made available to the public at the end of 1959, Bethlehem released an album called *Nina Simone and Her Friends*. Unbeknownst to Simone, Bethlehem had taken the three songs recorded back in 1957, at Simone's first session, and intended for use on *Side Street/Little Girl Blue*. Bethlehem had ultimately ditched these songs, but now included them on this new album. The previously unpublished tracks—"For All We Know," "African Mailman," and "He's Got the Whole World in His Hands"—were featured along with a reprise of "I Loves You Porgy." The record also contained songs by Chris Connor and Carmen McRae.

Simone, understandably, was infuriated that everybody seemed to be making money from her music but her. "The further I got into the business side of the music industry, the less I liked it," she wrote. "Unlike most artists I didn't care that much about a career as a popular singer. I was different— I was going to be a classical musician. Even after 'Porgy' hit, even after I signed to Colpix, it was all to raise money for proper tuition." Simone felt a strong disdain for show business, and she didn't hesitate to admit it for the duration of her career. "I wouldn't have missed the life because I hate it anyway; the cheap crooks, the disrespectful audiences, the way most people were so easily satisfied by dumb, stupid tunes." (*I Put a Spell on You*, 65) Indeed, some have suggested that Simone was never comfortable in the industry because she never quite overcame her mother's opinion of jazz— "the devil's music."

But Simone's popularity was mushrooming. *The Amazing Nina Simone* is a wildly eclectic album that received excellent critical reviews, but critics grappled with how to categorize Simone. "Children, Go Where I Send You," a rousing spiritual, follows a jazz standard, "Blue Prelude." Jazz legend Benny Goodman's hard-swinging "Stompin' at the Savoy" follows an English folk ballad, "Tomorrow (We Will Meet Once More)." Side one finishes off with a Rodgers and Hammerstein staple,

"It Might as Well Be Spring" (from *State Fair*), and a rhythm and blues song, "You've Been Gone Too Long." Side two is equally varied, with ballads, folk tunes, and a theme from a motion picture. "Drawing upon every idiom, blending the obvious trickery of a great performer and the secret formulas of a musical magician, Nina has put herself to the test," enthuse the liner notes. ". . . Everything that can be said in the musical idiom within the boundaries of the twelve numbers so carefully selected is here said—by Nina Simone." (Caras, 1)

Simone performed blues, show tunes, work songs, ballads, gospel, African chants, rhythm and blues, and soul, often seamlessly fusing them together. She sang, whispered, and moaned, sweetly and sensuously, but also wailed, screeched, bellowed, and shouted. Her music evoked raw and pure emotion. "Beneath the complex layers of her voice and her playing are longing, loss and happiness laid bare," writes one listener. (Gilmore, 1) And all of this on top of a classical piano sensibility and virtuosity. The likes of her had probably never been heard before. As John Wilson wrote in 1960, Simone "defies easy classification."

Still, many critics were quick to group her with other jazz singers. She often was compared to Billie Holiday, whose version of "I Loves You Porgy" inspired Simone's own. But Simone rejected this simple comparison, saying in one interview with Brantley Bardin, "She was a drug addict! They only compared me to her because we were both black—they never compared me to [the operatic legend] Maria Callas, and I'm more of a diva like her than anybody else." She resented the label of jazz singer, calling it racist: "To most white people, jazz means black and jazz means dirt and that's not what I play. . . . I play black classical music." (Bardin, 1)

Simone never liked being categorized or classified. In a 1968 interview with Michael Smith, she said, "I've been called the High Priestess—and I like that. But I just haven't got the words to describe what I do. It's like love. How do you talk about love?" (Roland, 109)

In her autobiography, Simone said, "If I had to be called something it should have been a folk singer, because there was more folk and blues than jazz in my playing. Whatever I was, the people in the Village liked it and word spread across the country." (*I Put a Spell on You*, 69) Sure enough, by early 1960, Simone had attracted a big jazz following. She had become the darling of the hip Greenwich Village music scene in New York, and she was regularly playing the bars there, including the Village Gate and the Village Vanguard. It was a time when there was wide interest in folk music and blues, too. And while jazz fans were exploring folk, fans of folk music were listening to jazz and blues. So Simone's distinct, uncategorizable style was appealing to all of these types of music fans. In a way, her music—like that of Bob Dylan— was ideally suited to the burgeoning scene in New York's Greenwich Village.

By early 1960, Simone had toured the country—including Chicago, Hollywood, and Pittsburgh—and finally had made some money on the Bethlehem records, so she moved into a bigger, more luxurious place and bought a Mercedes. People were recognizing her on the street and lavishing her with praise. She was hobnobbing with celebrities at parties and receiving lots of attention from male admirers. She had some new friends, including the folksinger Odetta, and she became acquainted with Langston Hughes, James Baldwin, and Leroi Jones (later known as Amiri Baraka). She was enjoying her new life very much. Simone was divorced from Don Ross at this point, but she was terribly busy with bookings.

A HYPNOTIC AND CONTROVERSIAL PERFORMER

Simone's live performances continued to draw huge, enthralled audiences, and they did so throughout her career. With her classical piano technique, emotional range, dignified

Odetta. As Simone gained popularity, she began to form friendships with other contemporary artists, such as Langston Hughes (with whom she created "Strange Fruit") and James Baldwin (who, like Simone, later went into exile). One of her great friends of that era was the Alabaman folk and blues singer Odetta, shown here in 1963. Odetta (1930–) is known for the gentleness and richness of her singing and for her unparalleled ability to communicate a song's meaning to her audience. She has worked for decades to keep the American folk and blues traditions alive.

manner, and almost regal bearing, Simone could hold live audiences in the palm of her hand. Even in her later years, Simone's audiences were mesmerized by her. "Simone perfected the art of hypnotizing an audience, using both intense musical emotion and absolute silence," writes author Lucy O'Brien. Why was she such a commanding performer? O'Brien adds, "[Simone] has been to the edge many times, fighting through marginalization, prejudice, and her personal torment to create something fierce with integrity." And, as critic Michael Smith once wrote, she could also pull fellow musicians into her spell. Smith was watching Simone perform at the Montreux Jazz Festival while he was sitting with the jazz greats Kenny Clarke, Art Taylor, Jack de Johnette, and Benny Bailey. "Musicians are not easily spellbound—but these four were completely captivated, and you could feel their common pride as they watched Nina Simone take what was a predominantly white (and initially indifferent) audience, and, by sheer artistry, by strength of character, and magical judgement, drive them into what can only be described as a mood of ecstatic acclamation." Smith continued, "Simone not only communicates, but she can create in an audience the need to receive and exalt in that communication. 'Now listen,' she says severely . . . and, like admonished children, the audience listens with rapt intensity." (Roland, 106)

Still, if those audiences weren't listening closely, Simone wouldn't hold back her indignation. As she had done very early in her career at the Midtown, she became incensed at an inattentive audience, and she would frequently chastise her listeners. Once, while performing in Harlem's Apollo Theater, she stopped playing to lecture her audience angrily about manners. When disrupted by the loud audience during a show at New York's Roundtable, she walked out. Not only did she refuse to go through with the other shows during that engagement, but she also sued the nightclub for $2,500. Photographer Burt Goldblatt writes that, at one of Simone's performances at the Newport Jazz Festival in 1966, "Simone told [the audience] to 'Shut up!' in order to quiet down when they had brought her back for an encore." Despite her brusque attitude, her presence was so commanding and music so powerful, that "she broke up that evening with a huge ovation from the crowd." (Goldblatt, 132)

Simone was developing a reputation for her determination, uncompromising integrity, and pride. She was a performer who demanded respect, and if she didn't receive it, she never hesitated to show her indignation. She was even known to harangue her musicians publicly. On one occasion in Antibes, France, she spontaneously sang an unexpected chorus in the middle of a piece, then openly and startlingly admonished her musicians for not keeping up with her.

In 1961, music critic Edward Kosner wrote in *The New York Post* that Simone was a "member of a new breed of Negro entertainer—the antithesis of the posturing 'Uncle Tom' who would do anything to win an audience's approval. . . . [Although she] wants the approval of an audience desperately . . . that approval must come on her terms and be grounded in respect for her work." (Kosner)

Regardless of the controversy surrounding Simone, the power of her music and personality was such that she continued to attract a loyal following. Nina Simone fans were diehard fans. She was able to connect with her live audiences in a profound way, and her shows became legendary.

MORE COLPIX ALBUMS

Colpix recognized the power of Simone's indisputably spellbinding performances and her unique rapport with her live audiences. The company quickly capitalized on her concert, club, and festival appeal. She recorded nine albums for Colpix in the early 1960s, and about half of these were live. At the time, she was one of the label's most profitable performers.

The Village Vanguard, 1967. Simone's fluid style and original improvisations sparked the interest of the growing folk-fan population in New York's Greenwich Village. She started playing at local bars and clubs like the Vanguard, a hotspot for folk music, and she attracted an entirely new audience. Her musical style defied categorization, just as she herself did, and it continued to evolve in the laid-back atmosphere of the Village.

Nina at Newport was recorded live at the Newport Jazz Festival on June 30, 1960, and released in 1961. It made the U.S. top thirty and is considered one of Simone's finest recordings. Its seven tracks include Cole Porter's "You'd Be So Nice to Come Home To," the African chant "Flo Me La," Dorothy Fields and Jimmy McHugh's "Porgy," the traditional tunes "Little Liza Jean" and "In the Evening by the Moonlight," Simone's own instrumental "Nina's Blues," and Richard Jones's "Trouble in Mind."

Another Simone standout, after 1961's *Forbidden Fruit*, was *Nina Simone at the Village Gate*, which was recorded in April 1961 and released in 1962. Simone always liked playing at the Gate in New York City, which she called "Jazz Central." "I was always treated properly at the Gate. Art D'Lugoff was the owner and we got to know each other well. Art treated performers as equals, as people worthy of respect. . . . He understood that respect was important: when it was due he gave it, and got it back in return." (*I Put a Spell on You*, 73) The live album begins with the Cole Porter standard "Just in Time." Simone's stirring, bluesy rendition of "House of the Rising Sun" was recorded by the British band The Animals soon thereafter and became a hit. Also included are her poignant version of Rodgers and Hart's "Too Good for Me," the upbeat eight-minutes-plus "Bye, Bye, Blackbird," and her evocative and ironic take on Oscar Brown, Jr.'s "Brown Baby."

Other albums from "the Colpix years" (1959–1964) include *Nina Sings Ellington* (1962), which contains eleven classic Ellington numbers, including "It Don't Mean a Thing (If It Ain't Got That Swing)"; a compilation album entitled *Nina's Choice* (1963); *Nina at Carnegie Hall* (1963), which was recorded in May 1963 and included Simone's own "If You Knew" and the traditional "Cotton-Eyed Joe"; *Folksy Nina* (1964), another live album from the same Carnegie Hall session; and *Nina Simone with Strings* (1966), which was also recorded in 1963 and included the Nina Simone/Herbert

Sacker song "Blackbird," the Gershwins' "Porgy, I Is Your Woman Now," and Rodgers and Hart's "Spring Is Here."

ANDY STROUD

In the summer of 1960, Simone met Andrew Stroud at one of her shows. Initially, Stroud told her that he was a bank teller. Simone was impressed with his look and his confidence, so when he invited her for a drink after the show, she accepted. The two started dating, and Simone quickly found out that he was, in fact, a police sergeant in Harlem. "On our first dates I realized his reputation when we went into a club or a bar. First of all everybody knew him and he knew everybody. Some guys would look up as he came into the room, check him, and just slide away without saying hello. . . . Andy was quiet and calm always, and always in control. That's what I liked most about him, that I felt safe when he was around. No one would dare to do anything to me with Andy there." He often brought her flowers and jewelry, and he was a solid, calming presence for Simone. "Andy came along and time slowed down when we were together and I could wind down: he relaxed me like a good massage." (*I Put a Spell on You*, 73)

Soon after Simone and Stroud became more serious and agreed to get married, she introduced him to her family. Her mother liked him, but her father was concerned about the fact that Andy had already been married three times before. He had reason to be worried.

A short while after Stroud met the Waymons, the couple went out one night to celebrate in Harlem. In her autobiography, Simone described how Stroud drank a lot of rum and then grew quiet. When a fan gave her a note, Stroud flew into a jealous rage and stormed out of the bar. That night, he physically abused Simone, striking her, tying her up, and holding her at gunpoint. Simone fled to a friend's house for two weeks. After he visited two psychiatrists and begged her to take him back, she decided to go through with the marriage. Simone wrote, "After years of being on my own travelling to clubs and halls all over America I can't describe how wonderful the idea of domestic life seemed to me at that moment. If I had turned him down I would be walking away from a security I hadn't felt since I was a little girl, since before Daddy got sick. . . . I forced myself to believe he wouldn't hit me any more." (*I Put a Spell on You*, 78)

The two were married on December 4, 1961, and they soon moved into a house in Mount Vernon, in the suburbs of New York. Stroud had three children from a previous marriage, so Simone became not only a wife but also a stepmother. Stroud retired from the police force and became Simone's full-time manager, handling all her bookings and deals. He was business-minded and organized. "Once I saw how he took to the work and the respect he got I trusted his judgement totally. It seemed like he was truly the man I'd dreamt of, the guy who'd swoop into my life to take care of me." Simone became pregnant within months of the move to Mount Vernon, and Lisa Celeste Stroud was born on September 12, 1962.

6

The Activist

1963–1966

The youth need to know the history of America. Since America is on top, they need to know what we did there, and so I'm happy that I'm still singing it.

— Nina Simone (quoted in Griffiths)

The birth of her daughter provided Simone with the longest break she'd had in a while, giving her time to think and reflect about her past, her priorities, her future. She wrote, "The responsibility of being a parent forces you to look at things differently... so as well as thinking about the future and trying to map it out with Andy, I started to take a more direct interest in the world around me, this world I had brought a child into." (*I Put a Spell on You*, 85) During this period, it seems that Simone finally relinquished her dreams of becoming a classical concert pianist. It was also when her political consciousness started to blossom.

Simone's defiance. Simone had experienced racism before, but after the assassination of Medgar Evers and the Birmingham bombing, her art became consciously and openly political. She became more critical of American society, and she often made her criticisms public at her concerts. Before long, she was known for heckling her audiences or even not showing up to perform. Still, many considered her voice one of the most important in expressing the black experience in America.

Simone was beginning to follow more closely the steps being taken in the struggle for civil rights in the United States. Many of her friends and colleagues from New York City and elsewhere—people like James Baldwin, Langston Hughes, and Odetta—were politically minded, and it slowly had begun to rub off on Simone. She started to consider the role that her race had played in her own life. She wrote, "I had not made a connection between the fights I had and any wider struggle for justice because of how I was raised: the Waymon way was to turn away from prejudice and to live your life as best you could, as if acknowledging the existence of racism was in itself a kind of defeat. . . .

Of course, I knew discrimination existed, but I didn't allow myself to admit it had any effect on me." (*I Put a Spell on You*, 86)

A year before Lisa's birth, Simone had attended a concert in Lagos, Nigeria, sponsored by the American Society of African Culture (AMSAC). Along with her friends Hughes and Baldwin, Simone was part of a group of around thirty African-American artists who celebrated the opening of a new cultural center in the African nation. At the time of the trip, Simone wasn't really involved in the civil rights movement, but something within her stirred. She wrote, "I felt for the first time the spiritual relaxation any Afro-American feels on reaching Africa.... I knew I'd arrived somewhere important and that Africa mattered to me, would always matter." (*I Put a Spell on You*, 80)

LORRAINE HANSBERRY'S INFLUENCE

It wasn't until she met Lorraine Hansberry, the author of the American classic play *A Raisin in the Sun* (1959)—the first play by an African-American woman ever to make it to Broadway— that Simone truly became engaged in the struggle for civil rights in the United States. Hansberry had an immense impact on Simone's social and political consciousness. Although the two had met before, they saw each other much more after Simone moved to Mount Vernon, which was just ten miles away from where Hansberry lived. They grew close, and their friendship was unlike any other Simone had experienced before: "We never talked about men or clothes or other such inconsequential things when we got together. It was always Marx, Lenin, and revolution. . . ." (*I Put a Spell on You*, 87)

Simone credited Hansberry with jump-starting her political education. "Through her I started thinking about myself as a black person in a country run by white people and a woman in a world run by men." (*I Put a Spell on You*, 87) Like many other African Americans (and others) in the United States, Simone had been following the events in the South ever since Rosa Parks's arrest in Montgomery, Alabama, in 1955 for refusing to give up her bus seat to a white man. She watched as Martin Luther King, Jr., organized the eleven-month-long Montgomery bus boycott, which resulted in a Supreme Court ruling that public bus segregation was unconstitutional. She saw the civil rights

LORRAINE HANSBERRY (1930–1965)

Lorraine Hansberry was the youngest of the four children of Carl and Nannie Hansberry, a successful middle-class African-American couple who lived in Chicago. Both of Hansberry's parents were intellectuals and activists, and such leading black figures as Langston Hughes, W.E.B. DuBois, and Paul Robeson visited the Hansberrys while Lorraine was growing up. She attended the University of Wisconsin, studied painting at the Art Institute of Chicago, and then moved to New York to pursue her writing career. Her first dramatic work, *A Raisin in the Sun* (the title is taken from a line in Langston Hughes's poem "Harlem"), is based on her family's experience of being the first blacks to move into a white neighborhood. The play, which Hansberry also adapted for the screen, focuses on the Younger family's struggles to hold on to their dignity and integrity in the face of discrimination. Hansberry became the youngest American and first black playwright to win the Best Play award from the New York Drama Critics Circle (1958–1959). It is widely considered a landmark of American theater.

Other plays written by Hansberry include *The Sign in Sidney Brustein's Window, Les Blancs, The Drinking Gourd*, and *What Use Are Flowers.* Before her early death from cancer in 1965, Hansberry also penned several articles on racism, homophobia, and other social and political issues. After her death, her ex-husband, Robert Nemiroff, completed *To Be Young, Gifted, and Black* (1969), a collage of Hansberry's poems, plays, letters, and other writings.

movement gain steam between 1961 and 1963, when more than a million demonstrators staged protests in the South against segregation and discrimination against blacks. She spoke about the movement more and more, often praising some of its leaders and participants during her performances. Still, it wasn't until early 1963, when her friendship with Hansberry was deepening, that Simone began to think about race and discrimination on a profound level and become more personally involved in the struggle.

The protests were nearing fever pitch in the spring of 1963, when King, the founder and head of the Southern Christian Leadership Council (SCLC) and a national figure by that time, joined the Reverend Fred Shuttlesworth and his Alabama Christian Movement for Human Rights (ACMHR), in the Birmingham campaign. Birmingham was the most vehemently anti-integrationist city in the South, and so this was a particularly significant battle. The campaign involved huge marches on City Hall; sit-ins at lunch counters, libraries, and churches; and a boycott on segregationist downtown merchants. Also, King delivered speeches to enormous audiences on nonviolent resistance. On April 12, King was arrested and sent to jail for violating the city's injunction against protests. After he wrote his famous "Letter from a Birmingham Jail," Hansberry phoned Simone, imploring her to take a more active role in the effort.

"MISSISSIPPI GODDAM"

On May 2, the campaign ended when Birmingham police and firefighters used dogs and firehoses against demonstrators, including many children. Over the next few days, people across the United States were horrified as they saw photographs of the brutality and violence used against the young black demonstrators; but the civil rights effort had achieved visibility at last. After the White House intervened, an agreement between SCLC representatives and Birmingham leaders finally was reached.

When President John F. Kennedy announced new civil rights legislation on June 11, Simone and many others were hopeful. But Medgar Evers, a leader in the movement, was murdered by his home in Jackson, Mississippi, on the very next day, and for Simone it all started to come crashing down. She was sad, angry, and disgusted. Then, a couple of months later, an incident occurred that seemed to push her over the edge.

On September 15, "[a]ll the truths that I had denied to myself for so long rose up and slapped my face. . . . I suddenly realized what it was to be black in America in 1963. . . . [I]t came as a rush of fury, hatred, and determination." (*I Put a Spell on You*, 89) Four black girls were killed when members of the Ku Klux Klan bombed the 16th Street Baptist Church in Birmingham, Alabama, where the girls had been attending a Bible class. Filled with fury, Simone felt that she had to do something.

In her 1968 interview with Michael Smith, Simone explained that after these two events occurred, she asked Stroud to teach her how to use a gun. She told Smith, "I'm not beyond killing— nobody is." Then, Smith writes, "She smiled broadly, and said, 'But I wrote "Mississippi Goddam" instead.'" (Roland, 110)

Simone turned her anguish, bitterness, anger, and passion into a powerful piece of music. In only an hour, she wrote what was to become an anthem for the civil rights movement. "It erupted out of me quicker than I could write it down," she wrote. (*I Put a Spell on You*, 90)

Alabama's gotten me so upset.
Tennessee made me lose my rest.
And everybody knows about Mississippi Goddam.

The writer and scholar Brian Ward has compared the song to Martin Luther King, Jr.'s "Letter from a Birmingham Jail," in which King responded to criticism that he was hoping for too much too quickly. King felt that blacks were tired of "deferring their rights until such time as whites saw fit to bestow them."

Ward wrote, "With its bold gospel-jazz chording and stentorian vocals, Simone's song perfectly captured the same mood of mounting impatience with white prevarication and false promises." (Ward, 301)

Like "Letter from a Birmingham Jail," the song's lyrics suggest that African Americans have waited long enough for equality in the United States:

> Don't tell me
> I'll tell you:
> Me and my people just about due.
> I been there, so I know.
> They keep on sayin', "Go slow."

The song speaks especially to the socialization of African-American children, who were led to believe that whites would treat them as equals if they behaved "correctly," or according to certain standards:

> Yes, you lied to me all these years.
> You told me to wash, and clean my ears,
> And talk real fine, just like a lady,
> And you'd stop calling me Sister Sadie.

The anti-American sentiment that appears throughout the song came to characterize Simone's later years, and the threat in "Mississippi Goddam" echoes threats in other Simone classics of her activist period:

> Oh, but this whole country is full of lies.
> You're all gonna die and die like flies.
> I don't trust you any more.
> You keep on saying, "Go slow!"

"Mississippi Goddam" closes by railing again against the

delays in desegregation and warning that the civil rights movement must not content itself with *gradual* progress. It is not a hopeful song; Simone seemed to think it unlikely that racial conflict in the United States could be resolved peacefully. One couplet in the song may best summarize her point of view: "You don't have to live next to me—/Just give me my equality."

After she composed "Mississippi Goddam," her first overtly political song, Simone became profoundly committed to fighting racism. She wrote, "I knew then that I would dedicate myself to the struggle for justice, freedom and equality under the law for as long as it took, until all our battles were won." (*I Put a Spell on You*, 90) She was infused with a new, raw sense of mission.

NINA SIMONE AND THE MOVEMENT

Simone's three-year "Philips period"—her years recording for the Philips label—began in 1964. Over the next decade, she publicly denounced American treatment of blacks, and much of her musical repertoire turned explicitly political. Her first album for Philips, *In Concert*, was recorded at Carnegie Hall in March of 1964. It included three of the songs of troubled romantic relationships she was known for—"I Loves You Porgy," "Don't Smoke in Bed," and "Plain Gold Ring." But it also included four expressly political offerings: the scathing, though rhythmically upbeat, "Mississippi Goddam," which not surprisingly had difficulty with distribution in the South; "Old Jim Crow," which she had cowritten, taking the songs of others and turning them into her own singular expression of the black experience; "Pirate Jenny," a number from Kurt Weill and Bertolt Brecht's *Threepenny Opera* (1928), which Simone relocates from London to the American South and in which she hisses, snarls, and vows revenge; and Dr. Alex Comfort's folk song "Go Limp," which she rearranged into a tale of the violence and threat of rape that went hand in hand with protest. One reviewer rightly calls *In Concert* "the most personal album that Simone issued during her stay on Philips in the mid-60s." (Erlewhine, 670)

The Birmingham bombing. One of the first events to really activate the civil rights movement was the bombing of the 16th Street Baptist Church in Birmingham, Alabama, in 1963. The bombing of the church, whose congregation was predominantly black, killed four schoolgirls and outraged activists who were already dissatisfied with the treatment of African-American people in the South. Simone wrote "Mississippi Goddam" in response to this bombing, and her song easily became an anthem of the movement and one of her signature pieces.

With the release of this album, Nina Simone had frankly and firmly announced herself as a gutsy musical proponent of civil rights. But by then she already had developed a reputation among civil rights workers by playing at fundraising events, appearing at marches, and performing for activists right on the frontlines in the South. In April 1963, she played at a mixed-race benefit concert at Miles College. A newspaper claimed that "her ululating rendition of Oscar Brown Jr.'s 'Brown Baby' had thousands cheering to the skies." (Ward, 301) She also performed at a Student Nonviolent Coordinating Committee (SNCC) benefit in April 1964 at Carnegie Hall, and that June, she headlined at an SNCC "Freedom Concert" in Westbury, New York. The Westbury concert was to raise money for the Mississippi Freedom Summer Project, an attempt by four civil rights groups to increase voter registration and establish a black political presence in Mississippi. By that summer, "Mississippi Goddam" had become an anthem for the activists. "I mean everybody in the Movement just sort of took that as a tribute to the Mississippi project," said Stanley Wise of the SNCC. (Ward, 301) Simone's music, and her formidable presence, continued to empower and energize the civil rights movement throughout the 1960s. The singer Bernice Johnson Reagon said, "Simone helped people to survive. . . . When you heard her voice on a record it could get you up in the morning. . . . She could sing anything, it was the sound she created. It was the sound of that voice and piano. . . . Nina Simone's sound captured the warrior energy that was present in the people. The fighting people." (Ward, 302)

In the spring of 1965, Simone decided at the last minute to play for the marchers walking from Selma to Montgomery, Alabama. Then she returned the following summer to perform for another march, even though she hadn't been scheduled. Later that year, the Congress of Racial Equality (CORE) honored Simone with a special award for her efforts on their behalf. H. Rap Brown, an SNCC leader and friend of Simone's, called her "the singer of the black revolution because there is no other singer who sings real protest songs about the race situation." (Ward, 302)

Throughout this time, Simone voiced her opinions to the press, never hesitant about showing her disapproval about certain race-related matters. In her autobiography, Simone described an incident in which she saw an off-Broadway play featuring two black actors in the cast. She felt that their roles were "insulting to black people," so in the middle of the show she went to the stage and told them so. She wrote, "When injustice stared me in the face I struck out fiercely, without taking time to consider the implications. . . . I was not cold and intellectual about campaigning, I was intuitive." (*I Put a Spell on You*, 97)

During this period, Simone counted Stokely Carmichael and the South African musician Miriam Makeba among her friends and admirers. When Simone first went to Philadelphia to meet Carmichael, he singled her out in the audience and hailed her as the true singer of the civil rights movement. She also met Louis Farrakhan, who went on to become a leading voice in the racial separatist movement in the United States. It was during this time that Simone realized and affirmed her own thoughts on separatism: "In the white man's world the black man would always lose out, so the idea of a separate black nation, whether it was in America or in Africa, made sense." (*I Put a Spell on You*, 100)

THE PHILIPS YEARS

Simone's musical output throughout the early to mid-1960s was all recorded on the Philips label, a subsidiary of Mercury Records. Simone wrote that Wilhelm Langenberg, the owner, had approached her (she called him "Big Willy") after he heard "Mississippi Goddam" in Holland and then listened to it "non-stop for fifty-two hours." (*I Put a Spell on You*, 106) She signed with him, and the two became close friends. She and Stroud would cross the Atlantic every year for ten years to attend Big Willy's extravagant and legendary New Year's parties. Simone wrote that Big Willy and his wife, Ena, were her and her husband's best friends in Europe. When Simone became embittered about the state of race relations in the world and "sometimes despair turned to hate of all things white," she said, "[i]t was the thought of men like Wilhelm Langenberg which saved me from bigotry, because he was impossible to hate." (*I Put a Spell on You*, 107)

Simone stayed on the Philips label through 1967, recording

seven albums. After *In Concert*, Philips released *Broadway-Blues-Ballads* (1964), a potpourri of Simone material (both live and studio-recorded) ranging from Broadway melodies, to ballads, to standards, to pop, to typically uncategorizable Simone fare. Of the Broadway tunes, there is "Something Wonderful" from *The King and I*; "Night Song" from *Golden Boy*, a 1964 musical that starred Sammy Davis, Jr.; and "Nobody," an ain't-it-awful classic popularized by the turn-of-the-century black vaudeville performer Bert Williams. The most popular track on the album at the time was "Don't Let Me Be Misunderstood," a rhythm-and-bluesy piece that quickly became a favorite for Simone fans but didn't actually hit the charts until the British group The Animals covered it in 1965. In the liner notes for the 1993 rerelease of the album, James Gavin writes, "An anguished plea for sympathy at a time of harsh action, the song is an obvious echo of the civil rights movement. The volatile singer found more than a touch of autobiography in its words. 'Don't you know no one alive can always be an angel?/When everything goes wrong you see some bad.'" (Gavin, 1) *Broadway-Blues-Ballads* also contains Simone's unforgettable, foot-stomping, hand-clapping, bluesy, and infectious "See-Line Woman."

Gavin felt that this album was an effort on the part of Philips to move Simone into the mainstream. He wrote, "As the civil rights struggle weighed upon Simone more and more heavily, the mahogany voice heard on her early albums began to show a few cracks, and her shows grew visibly harsher and angrier. Protest songs started to dominate her repertoire, as they would for the rest of the decade. Most of *Broadway-Blues-Ballads* is an attempt to take Simone beyond her cult status by presenting her as a mainstream pop singer." (Gavin, 1)

And there's no doubt that as Simone became increasingly political, she began to lose some of her audience. Author Lucy O'Brien writes, "Nina was shunned by the mainstream when she began playing SNCC shows." "It was no accident," Simone told O'Brien, "that most active black musicians couldn't get major label deals in the late 1960s and '70s." (O'Brien, 88)

Certain U.S. audiences didn't know how to respond to Nina Simone. Her rhetoric and her songs became more militant and intense. Reviewing one of her performances at the annual Newport Jazz Festival, a trade paper said, "The audience didn't know whether they were being entertained or lectured." (Goldblatt, 100) But true Nina Simone devotees continued to flock to her shows, buy her albums, and fall under her spell.

Simone's next album released by Philips was *I Put a Spell on You* (1965). The title track was written and originally recorded by Screamin' Jay Hawkins. Although some of Simone's music was acquiring more of a soul and rhythm and blues tilt, the album was still dramatic, eclectic, and surprising. O'Brien writes, "Simone's version of the Screamin' Jay Hawkins original 'I Put a Spell on You' still chills with its intense overtones of desperation, charm, and voodoo." (O'Brien, 89) "Ne Me Quitte Pas," Simone's heart-rending and highly personal interpretation of the Jacques Brel original, also became a favorite of Simone fans throughout the years. The LP includes two other French songs, written by Charles Aznavour ("You've Got to Learn" and "Tomorrow Is My Turn"); the provocative "Gimme Some" (written by Simone's husband, Andy Stroud) and "Take Care of Business"; and "One September Day," which was written by Rudy Stevenson, Simone's guitarist.

Pastel Blues (1966), recorded in May 1965, followed *I Put a Spell on You.* This album was much more subdued than her previous Philips recordings, and a stark bitterness permeated it. She performed a devastating rendition of poet Lewis Allen's "Strange Fruit," a song about Southern lynchings that Billie Holiday had made famous. Simone also interpreted one of Holiday's own riveting compositions, "Tell Me More and More and Then Some." The LP also includes "Trouble in Mind," the heartbreaking "End of the Line," and the bluesy "Nobody Knows You When You're Down and Out." Andy

Nina at Newport. Simone often played jazz festivals during the 1960s, even though she rejected the label of jazz musician. The annual Newport Jazz Festival was one of her standards, and she is known to have "lectured" her audiences there several times. Her in-concert protests against the racial inequalities of American life became stronger as the civil rights movement gained momentum. At the same time, the soulful yearning of her music expressed the sadness beneath the anger.

Stroud contributed "Be My Husband," his adaptation of a blues chant. The thrilling, ten-minute-long Simone version of the traditional "Sinnerman" has become a Simone classic and was used in the film *The Thomas Crown Affair* (2000). Simone once said that she liked only five of her albums, "one of them being *Pastel Blues.*" (Roland, 110)

By the time *I Put a Spell on You* and *Pastel Blues* were

released, Simone had developed a strong following in Europe, primarily in France and England. The title track from *I Put a Spell on You* even made it onto the British charts. Simone went on to receive coverage in the British press when The Animals covered "Don't Let Me Be Misunderstood." In the same year, Simone made her first concert tour of Europe, and she won over audiences in the United Kingdom when she debuted in London. She wrote that during her first visit to London, she, Stroud, and Lisa thoroughly enjoyed being away from the United States. Simone had been growing more and more disillusioned by the race situation in her home country. The radical Black Power leader Malcolm X had been murdered in February 1965, and there were race riots in New York City; Jacksonville, Florida; and Chicago. So when she and her family arrived in London, "We did the kinds of things normal tourists do and tried to kid ourselves that America didn't exist," Simone later recalled. (*I Put a Spell on You*, 105)

In Antibes, in southern France, French audiences were equally smitten with Simone, and she drew raves for her performance at the Montreux Jazz Festival. Simone's trips to Europe became more frequent, and she found that her audiences were considerably more receptive than those back in the United States. She said in an interview with Michael Smith, "People in Europe are so well informed. They seem to know all of my records and when they were made. . . . I suppose the Civil Rights thing does come into it, and has some bearing on their response, but in a lot of cases I'm sure it has nothing to do with it." (Roland, 109)

DISILLUSIONMENT

Simone also found that some of her European fans had been familiar with several of her earlier songs that had never, to her knowledge, been recorded. It was then that she realized the extent to which her music had been bootlegged. She wrote, "I knew that all artists were exploited in this way, but how come black artists always seemed to get ripped off more often, more extensively, than white?" (*I Put a Spell on You*, 105)

In early 1966, Simone met up with some of her friends involved in the civil rights movement, including Stokely Carmichael. By this time, Simone had solidly aligned herself with the Black Power movement. She wrote, "I talked to Stokely and read their manifesto. I agreed with every word: I just wish some of the opponents of Black Power had bothered to read it too, because they would have understood that Black Power was a lot more than black men with guns—it was a way of returning the black man's pride." (*I Put a Spell on You*, 109)

In the spring of that year, Carmichael became chairman of the SNCC, and CORE adopted the Black Power platform. The SCLC and Dr. Martin Luther King, Jr., of course, still adhered to their doctrine of nonviolence, but Simone no longer believed in this approach. After King was stabbed in Chicago, Simone wrote, "I was tired of our leaders having to risk their lives each time they went out on the street, tired of being asked to turn the other cheek each time my race was subjected to another indignity. I, for one, was through with turning the other cheek, through with loving my enemies." (*I Put a Spell on You*, 110)

Simone was entering a strange and difficult period of her life. She was embittered, resentful, sad, angry, and confused. And she was beginning to lose all faith in the movement and in the United States. Moreover, both her personal life and her behavior on stage were growing increasingly erratic.

The High Priestess of Soul

1967–1969

. . . [T]he world is big—
Big and bright and round—
And it's full of folks like me
Who are black, yellow, beige, and brown.

— Langston Hughes/Nina Simone,
"Backlash Blues"

Toward the end of the 1960s, Simone's disappointment, bitterness, and anger over the treatment of African-American people in the United States, along with general exhaustion from a grueling touring and recording schedule, all started to take a serious toll on her. She was mourning the loss of both her friend Lorraine Hansberry, who had died of cancer in 1965, and the radical civil rights leader Malcolm X; she was enraged about police brutality against African Americans; and she was generally dismayed about the state of affairs in the country. The United

A new complexity. It was during the late 1960s that Simone really matured as a performer. With the assassination of Dr. Martin Luther King, Jr., the political climate became even more charged, and Simone understood that there might be no nonviolent way to resolve American racial tensions. Her performances began to take on a new complexity— angry, sad, militant, resigned, and infinitely wise all at once. This photograph, taken thirty years later, gives an idea of Simone's commanding presence at the keyboard.

States was entering a particularly turbulent time, and, in a way, Simone's outlook was mirroring that of the entire nation.

TOUGH TIMES AND TRIUMPHS

During her tour with Bill Cosby at the end of 1966 and the beginning of 1967, Simone experienced some disconcerting and queer moments. "My mind would leave entirely and I'd sit staring at nothing, unaware of time going by until some noise snapped me out of it. I was in a state where I was half outside myself, observing my peculiar behavior from a safe distance."

She describes an incident during the tour when "Andy walked into my dressing room and found me staring into the mirror putting make-up in my hair, brown make-up, because I wanted to be the same color all over." (*I Put a Spell on You*, 110) Stroud was frightened and concerned that something was seriously wrong with Simone. Her musicians noticed her strange behavior, too, but she managed to get through the tour.

Still, throughout her difficult times, she was almost always able to sustain an almost holy command over her audiences for the duration of her career. In spite of Simone's bizarre state of mind, the Cosby tour was an enormous success, as had been several of her other recent performances. At the 1966 Newport Jazz Festival, she had received a standing ovation from the audience of fifteen thousand. That year she also had been voted Woman of the Year by the Jazz at Home Club. Stephen Holden wrote in *The New York Times*, "Rooted in extreme emotional ambivalence, her performances have the aura of sacramental rites, in which a priestess and her flock work to establish a musical communion." (Brennan, 229) Indeed, her audiences were like her congregants, and her fellow musicians nick-named her "the High Priestess of Soul"—a sobriquet that Simone herself never accepted. (Harrington, C01)

The year 1966 had seen the release of two more albums with Philips: *Let It All Out* and *Wild Is the Wind*. The former contained cover versions of Bob Dylan's "Ballad of Hollis Brown," Van McCoy's "For Myself," Irving Berlin's "This Year's Kisses," and the Billie Holiday classic "Don't Explain." Other highlights include "The Other Woman," "Mood Indigo," and "Images." *Wild Is the Wind* standouts are stirring versions of the previously recorded folk song "Black Is the Color of My True Love's Hair" and "Lilac Wine" and the moving, beautiful title track, an old movie theme. The selections "Why Keep on Breaking My Heart?," "Break Down and Let It All Out," and "I Love Your Lovin' Ways" are "poppier" and more like rhythm and blues. But the most memorable track from this LP is of

Simone's own composition: "Four Women." This powerful lament about four black women of differing gradations of skin tone created considerable controversy, but it also became a show favorite. It was banned in New York and Philadelphia on charges that it was insulting to black women. Simone, though, said that she wrote "Four Women" to bring about some discussion about how black women fell victim to white standards of beauty. She wrote in her autobiography, "All the song did was to tell what entered the minds of most black women in America when they thought about themselves: their complexions, their hair—straight, kinky, natural, which?—and what other women thought of them. Black women didn't know what the hell they wanted because they were defined by things they didn't control, and until they had the confidence to define themselves they'd be stuck in the same mess forever—that was the point the song made. . . . The song told a truth that many people in the USA— especially black men—simply weren't ready to acknowledge at that time." (*I Put a Spell on You*, 117) As always, Simone didn't refrain from expressing her opinions, regardless of how certain people could be expected to react.

High Priestess of Soul (1967) was her last album released with the Philips label. The album mixed some gospel pieces (the traditional "Take Me to the Water"), some jazz-inflected work ("Work Song" by Nat Adderley and Oscar Brown, Jr.), and a few pop songs (Chuck Berry's "Brown-Eyed Handsome Man" and Bobby Scott's "Don't Pay Them No Mind"). These are topped off with Simone's own "Come Ye," which, in the liner notes to the CD release, Joel Siegel calls "particularly inspired and inspiring, a visionary voice-and-percussion rallying cry reaffirming survival, unity and peace." (Siegel, 1)

Yet Simone's personal crisis continued throughout 1967 and 1968. She was feeling alienated from the movement and experiencing a growing sense of isolation in general. She felt suffocated by the demands of her career and her obligations to all those involved. She started missing shows, and she drank alcohol more frequently. Although she was still receiving critical acclaim—she was voted Female Jazz Singer of the Year by the National Association of Television and Radio Announcers in 1967—she was unpredictable in concert, and some audiences and critics didn't know how to respond to her increasingly eccentric onstage behavior. Some people were put off as well by her militancy. Burt Goldblatt describes how, at a 1967 performance for the Newport Jazz Festival, she played a rendition of "Backlash Blues," a Langston Hughes poem set to music. "She held the audience and dramatically dug in deep with [the song], which she transformed into a biting piece of expressive agony," he said. "It made you wince." (Goldblatt, 144)

On April 4, 1968, Simone was preparing for a gig at the Westbury Music Fair on Long Island, New York, when she learned that Dr. Martin Luther King, Jr., had been slain at a hotel in Memphis, Tennessee. Nevertheless, she performed on April 7. She wrote, "I think my performance that night was one of my very best, focused by the love and quiet despair we all felt at our loss." (*I Put a Spell on You*, 115) She played "Why? (The King of Love Is Dead)." The devastated Simone had written the song with Gene Taylor, her bass player, in tribute to Dr. King. Her performance that night, which was recorded for her album *'Nuff Said!*, was riveting, with her passion, sorrow, and rage evident. During the monologue that introduces the King tribute, Simone can be heard saying to the audience, "I ain't about to be nonviolent, honey."

Soon after the Westbury performance, she left for a tour of Europe. She performed in Amsterdam, Rotterdam, and then at the Montreux Festival, where she found herself crying onstage at her piano. "The true weight of the last month's events hit me," she wrote. (*I Put a Spell on You*, 115) She felt that the movement had fallen apart. Many of its leaders were dead, imprisoned, or under FBI surveillance. Her friend H. Rap Brown had been shot and wounded and convicted on a firearms charge, and then had gone into hiding. Stokely

STOKELY CARMICHAEL (1942–1998)

Born in Trinidad, Carmichael moved to New York City in 1952, where he attended high school. In 1960, he enrolled at Howard University and joined the Student Nonviolent Coordinating Committee (SNCC) soon after. He was one of the Freedom Riders, intrepid black and white civil rights workers who rode buses side by side in the Deep South to desegregate them. Unprotected by police, Carmichael was one of many men who were beaten up by white mobs, and the Riders were arrested when they arrived at their destinations. He claimed to have been arrested so many times that after 32, he lost count. When his leadership skills became apparent, he was named chairman of SNCC in 1966. In June 1966, a group of rights volunteers, including Carmichael and Dr. Martin Luther King, Jr., joined together to complete James Meredith's march after he was shot and wounded. Following his arrest, Carmichael gave his famous Black Power speech, where he declared, "We been saying freedom for six years, and we ain't got nothin'. What we gonna start saying now is 'Black Power.'" He called for black people to unite, claim their heritage, and reject American values once and for all. He also advocated Afrocentric fashions and styles. Black Power became the mantra of CORE, but Carmichael's beliefs split the SNCC. He openly criticized Dr. King's nonviolent tactics and was accused of being a racist. In 1967, he cowrote *Black Power: The Politics of Black Liberation* with Charles Hamilton. Carmichael eventually joined the radical militant group the Black Panthers. When he opposed some of the group's platforms, he moved to Guinea, Africa, where he founded the All-African People's Revolutionary Party and changed his name to Kwame Toure. He died of cancer in 1998.

Simone signs with RCA. Simone left Philips and signed with RCA in 1967, beginning a string of hit albums and a phase of great commercial success. Andy Stroud, her husband and manager, was pushing her harder and harder to make the most of the success of her European tour and her contract with RCA. But she had begun to feel that the civil rights movement had lost its momentum, and she was losing faith that there would ever be an equilibrium between black people and white people in the United States. She produced another civil rights anthem—a sadder one—"To Be Young, Gifted, and Black."

Carmichael was in and out of prison; like his brother John, Robert Kennedy had been murdered. Simone wanted to cancel the tour, but Stroud convinced her to press on. Four tracks were recorded at Montreux and three in Rome in June 1968, with Simone's brother Sam on piano.

RCA RECORDS

Stroud pushed Simone because he wanted to capitalize on her growing popularity in Europe. Since she had switched from Philips to RCA Records in 1967, she had begun her most successful commercial phase. *Nina Simone Sings the Blues* and *Silk & Soul*, both released in 1967, were her first releases with RCA. This time, her albums weren't just drawing critical acclaim; they were also selling. Highlights of *Nina Sings the Blues* include "Since I Fell for You," the sultry Simone classic "I Want a Little Sugar in My Bowl," and the traditional "House of the Rising Sun." Simone wrote or cowrote four other numbers on the album, and Stroud contributed "Buck." *Silk & Soul* included Burt Bacharach's "The Look of Love" and Billy Taylor's "I Wish I Knew How It Would Feel to Be Free," along with "Turn Me On." The music seemed to be geared more to pleasing the mainstream than the music of her earlier albums: "Simone was not as well-served by her tenure with RCA in the late '60s and early '70s, another prolific period which saw the release of nine albums. These explored a less eclectic range, with a considerably heavier pop-soul base to both the material and arrangements." (Erlewhine, 1020) Still, *'Nuff Said*, released in 1968, went on to receive an Emmy nomination. On top of her compelling performance of "Why? (The King of Love Is Dead)," the album also included "Ain't Got No/I Got Life" from the musical *Hair* (1968). It was released as a single in the United Kingdom and actually reached number two on the pop charts. The LP also contained "Backlash Blues," "Sunday in Savannah," and the traditional spiritual "Take My Hand, Precious Lord."

Stroud wanted Simone to ride that wave of success in Europe, but she felt that he was pushing her too hard. She wrote, "We weren't communicating any more, and he was making decisions as my manager rather than as my husband." (*I Put a Spell on You*, 116) Simone was exhausted, and she wanted to spend time by herself and with her daughter, Lisa. She felt her marriage tearing at the seams, and her behavior at her shows became more belligerent. Writer David Nathan describes a concert in the packed London Palladium at which she asked that all the black people in the audience stand up. "This show is just for you!" she said to them, thereby alienating and angering many of the white Simone fans in the crowd. (Nathan, 56)

In the next year, 1969, *To Love Somebody* was released, and again a track from the album reached the British top ten—the title song, written by Barry and Robin Gibb. The album also offered three Bob Dylan covers, including Simone's classic version of "I Shall Be Released," as well as Leonard Cohen's "Suzanne" and "Revolution," another protest song, written by Simone and Weldon Irvine, Jr. In the introduction to "Revolution," Simone can be heard scolding her musicians: "Hold it! This is louder than usual. Let it groove on its own thing." In her 1968 interview with Michael Smith, when Smith asked her whether it was true that she was difficult to work with, she responded, "Yes. I demand of my musicians what I demand of myself. I set very high standards because I'm a musician myself. Maybe, just once in a while, I might really please myself, but more often, I don't. There is always something you could have done better." (Roland, 109)

Six months after *To Love Somebody* came out, RCA issued *Black Gold*, a live recording of a show at Philharmonic Hall in New York. This album contains one of the all-time Simone classics, "To Be Young, Gifted, and Black," Simone's tribute to her deceased friend Lorraine Hansberry; the title was taken from a work of Hansberry's that was published posthumously. The song celebrates the creative potential of black youth:

> To be young, gifted and black—
> Oh what a lovely precious dream!
> To be young, gifted and black—
> Open your heart to what I mean.
> In the whole world, you know,
> There are a billion boys and girls
> Who are young, gifted, and black,
> And that's a fact!

CORE had declared the song to be the "black national anthem," something that made Simone very proud "because it showed I was succeeding as a protest singer, that I was writing songs people remembered and were inspired by." (*I Put a Spell on You*, 109) The album also boasts impressive versions of "Black Is the Color of My True Love's Hair," "Westwind," and Sandy Denny's "Who Knows Where the Time Goes?"

Although RCA was churning out Simone's albums, she was still concerned about the lack of progress toward racial equality in the United States. "The days when revolution really had seemed possible were gone forever. I watched the survivors run for cover in community and academic programmes and felt betrayed, partly by our own leaders but mostly by white America. And I felt disgusted by my own innocence." (*I Put a Spell on You*, 118) Furthermore, she was arguing continually with Stroud. Simone decided it was time for a change—a drastic one.

The Expatriate

1970–1978

I left this country because I didn't like this country. I didn't like what it was doing to my people, and I left.

—Nina Simone, quoted in *Jet*, April 22, 1985

In 1970, Nina Simone was ready to take a break. She was disgusted with the racial inequality she saw in the United States, yet she also was disillusioned with the civil rights movement and hopeless about the possibility of change. She believed that the movement had lost its focus and failed to achieve its goals. As recently as 1997, Simone said, "I think [the state of race relations in the United States] is hopeless for the majority of black people. I think the rich are too rich and the poor are too poor. I don't think the black people are going to rise at all; I think most of them are going to die." (Powell, 1)

Nina in exile. Nina Simone had been performing practically nonstop since her first gigs in Atlantic City in 1954, and by the early 1970s she needed a break. She left her husband and her country and traveled around the world—notably to Barbados, where she became involved with the prime minister, and to Liberia. She took time away from the music industry, too, in an effort to determine what she wanted to do with her life. It was a rocky period for her. This photograph shows Simone on an Israeli beach in 1978.

Simone realized that her devotion to the movement had led her to neglect other parts of her life. "I had presumed we could change the world and had run down a dead-end street leaving my career, child and husband way behind, neglected," she writes. (*I Put a Spell on You*, 118) She felt that she needed some time off, but Stroud didn't think that was a good idea. They argued about this. "As usual he refused to accept that I needed rest, and I realized he wasn't even sure I meant it. That did it." (119)

BARBADOS

She *did* mean it. She walked out on Stroud and fled to Barbados, leaving Lisa with Stroud's mother. In Barbados, she swam and dived, feeling far removed from her career, her troubles with Stroud, and the United States in general. Simone claimed that her choice to leave Stroud was only "to show him I was serious about needing rest and that, if he wouldn't give it to me, then, hell, I'd take it anyway." (*I Put a Spell on You*, 120) But when, after her rest, she returned to their Mount Vernon house, she found that he had packed his bags and gone. The house was empty.

After the trip to Mount Vernon, Simone returned to Barbados for a few weeks, had an affair with a hotel porter, and generally relaxed. She returned to the United States soon afterward to tend to some matters and perform a few concerts. She now was facing financial and legal problems in addition to her personal problems. The IRS claimed that she was withholding money and wasn't cooperating; her record label wasn't comfortable with her political views; and she even had a falling out with her father. She went so far as to tell him that she disowned him. Simone felt betrayed by everyone—the show business industry, white America, the civil rights movement, her country, her husband, and her father.

When she learned that her father had prostate cancer and that his condition was deteriorating, she stayed with her mother, but still she refused to see him. Simone wrote that by the time he died of prostate cancer, "I felt nothing, nothing at all. I wasn't cold or indifferent to his death; it was as if my ability to experience emotion had been cut out of me and I was dead inside." A week later, her sister Lucille died, also of cancer. She wrote, "I turned to stone inside. . . . What sort of person was I when sometimes I could cry for hours without knowing why and yet couldn't find a tear for Daddy and my beloved Lucille? What sort of person could break down and cry on stage in Europe over the deaths of political leaders and then refuse to visit her father's grave?" When she returned to Barbados this time, she said, "I fled . . . pursued by ghosts: Daddy, Lucille, the movement, Martin [Luther King, Jr.], Malcolm [X], my marriage, my hopes." (*I Put a Spell on You*, 128)

Thus began Nina Simone's self-imposed exile from the country of her birth. While she was living in Barbados, she was able to spend some time with her daughter, Lisa, something she hadn't been able to do while touring. She became the mistress of the prime minister of Barbados, Earl Barrow, and she and Lisa lived for a while on the grounds of his estate. In the meantime, her divorce from Stroud was finalized. Yet because Stroud had managed Simone's career, her finances and business affairs had fallen into shambles. She often made trips back to the United States, staying in a rented apartment in New York City, to try to put things in order.

QUITTING THE MUSIC BUSINESS

It was also during this time, around 1971, that Simone recorded *Here Comes the Sun* and *Emergency Ward!*. The title track off of the first album is an impressive rendition of the classic Beatles tune, but the LP also contains a stunning version of Stan Vincent's "Ooh, Child," Bob Dylan's "Just Like a Woman," a moving "Mr. Bojangles," and Jacques Revaux's "My Way." *Emergency Ward!*, which was recorded in 1971 and 1972 and released in 1972, combines a live performance with a studio session. It includes covers of George Harrison's "Isn't It a Pity" and "My Sweet Lord."

Simone's younger brother Sam worked as her manager for a while. During this period, her performances received mixed reviews. Some critics resented Simone's bitterness and felt alienated and let down by her. They couldn't make sense of her behavior, and her disillusionment with show business was becoming very evident. In 1971, Mike Jahn of *The New York Times* wrote, "It is easy for Nina Simone to be a magnificent artist. She has been many times. It is just as easy for her to be proud and dignified, in keeping both with the level of her artistry, and with the richness of the culture of which she is so justly proud. Why she chose not to do so is unfathomable and sad." (Brennan, 230) John Rockwell offered a much more favorable viewpoint: "Miss Simone's unwillingness to compromise, artistically, financially, or personally, can be seen as heroic—as the firm refusal of an artist, a woman, and a black, to bow to forces she feels are threatening her." (Brennan, 230)

Simone's last album with RCA, recorded in 1974, was appropriately entitled *It Is Finished*. It contains the classic "Mr. Bojangles," "Let It Be Me," a cover of Ike and Tina Turner's "Funkier Than a Mosquito's Tweeter," and the spiritual "Come by Here." She'd had enough of the industry, and after *It Is Finished*, she left the business for some time. Simone wrote, "My record deals expired along with my marriage and I became one more black artist 'difficult to place' in the neat world the labels created. . . . Nina Simone was walking away from an industry with no place for her, an industry which had been happy to sell millions of her records through the sixties and then turned around and said they didn't think people wanted to listen to those kinds of records anymore." (*I Put a Spell on You*, 136)

Still, that year also brought a tremendous honor for Simone: On May 11, she was the guest of honor at the annual Human Kindness Day celebration. One hundred thousand African-American people were in attendance at the six-hour concert held at the Washington Monument in the nation's capital, where Simone was given a citation by Muhammad Ali and saluted at a dinner at the Smithsonian Institution. "I was proud to be saluted in this way by my own people, the people I cared most about, but it didn't change the way I felt about America." (*I Put a Spell on You*, 136)

Around this time, she felt a general willingness to perform but also an overwhelming uncertainty: "Nowadays, I'll do isolated performances when the time and money is right, but no more nonstop tours. . . . Right now I'm trying to decide exactly what I want to do with my life. I need some time to work it out. . . . " (Nathan, 59) One of those isolated performances was a show at the Lincoln Center, just a few months after Human Kindness Day. Simone continued to be as outspoken and imperious as ever: "She spoke of how the U.S. will let her get all the fame she wants, but no money." (Nathan, 59)

Simone's personal troubles mounted when the IRS and Mount Vernon authorities confiscated and sold her house, which had been neglected and fallen into disrepair. Her relationship with Earl Barrow was failing, as well. Unsure where to turn or what to do next, she followed the advice of her friend Miriam Makeba and, with Lisa, now twelve years old, moved to Liberia.

LIBERIA

Simone hadn't been back to Africa since her trip with AMSAC in 1961. She was thrilled with the idea of returning to West Africa, which she called "the home of my ancestors before slavery, when they were free. . . ." "Liberia and America were connected through history in a positive way," she wrote, "and Liberian culture and society reflected that. It was a good place to start for any Afro-American looking to reconcile themselves to their own history." (*I Put a Spell on You*, 138)

Upon arrival in Liberia, Simone, Lisa, and Makeba were taken to the Presidential Palace, where they were the guests of honor at a party. During the first week there, they attended a different party every night. Simone also went on the first of several dates that Makeba arranged for her. She felt an immediate, and unprecedented, sense of belonging in Liberia. When asked how she felt when she arrived in Africa, she replied, "That I was at home. I took off my shoes and walked in the dirt streets, smelled all the smells. . . . They didn't even want me to sing over there, they just wanted me to have a good time! I felt thoroughly at home there." (Bardin)

In fact, Simone felt so comfortable that during her first week there, she danced naked in a club for two hours. She later wrote that on the third night of her visit, she "started dancing, and the champagne and my happiness and the music got to me all at once, got to me good. I started stripping my clothes

THE FOUNDING OF LIBERIA

In 1821, the American Colonization Society sponsored the landing of some settlers on the coast of Liberia. The Society was a group of American abolitionists who helped blacks return to Africa, believing that this would solve the issue of slavery and what they viewed as the essential incompatibility of the white and black races. The blacks were granted possession of the land by local chiefs of the De tribe. Eventually, almost fifteen thousand African Americans migrated to Liberia. By 1839, the settlers had established a commonwealth and elected a governor, Thomas Buchanan, a black cousin of American President James Buchanan. In 1847, Liberia became a fully independent republic. Joseph Jenkins Roberts of Virginia became the first elected president. Although the Americo-Liberians made up a small minority of the population, they dominated the ruling class, and, ironically, the darker-skinned indigenous population was denied equal rights with their lighter-skinned Americo-Liberian counterparts. By the American Civil War, the migration to Liberia had virtually come to a standstill.

off while I danced, and everybody started clapping, hooting, feeding me champagne. I got down to nothing at all and danced naked for at least two hours, having the time of my life." (*I Put a Spell on You*, 140)

Simone's time in Liberia was also positive in that she and Lisa "had a chance to try and behave like an average mother and daughter." (*I Put a Spell on You*, 151) She also dated several men during her two-year stay. But in 1976, Simone began thinking seriously about where to educate Lisa. She found a school she liked in Switzerland and enrolled Lisa. Soon, though, she realized she wanted to be near her daughter—so she moved to Switzerland to join her.

EUROPE

After her wonderful experiences in Liberia, Simone found it difficult to adjust to life in Switzerland. She missed her friends, she missed the climate, and she felt lonely. On a whim, she flew down to Liberia to visit a former lover, and she ended up meeting a Liberian man who invited her to accompany him to London. The two weren't involved romantically; rather, he offered to help her to restart her career. When she found out that he wasn't paying for her hotel room, as he'd promised to do, she confronted him and they argued. He beat her, and she fell to the floor, unconscious. All alone in London, and with no money left—her room had been ransacked, perhaps by the same con man who beat her—Simone was so miserable that she attempted suicide by swallowing sleeping pills.

After regaining consciousness in the hospital, Simone decided that she needed to take charge of her life. So, with no manager or lawyer in Europe, she began to perform live again for the first time in years. She spent the next two years playing small gigs in Holland, Germany, France, and Switzerland. When Andy Stroud called her unexpectedly and offered to be her manager for a small American tour, she took him up on the offer. It was to be strictly business, and Simone had great faith

A love affair with France. In the later years of her life, after years of racial tension and a number of brushes with the law had motivated her to leave the United States, Simone spent most of her time in France. She appreciated the size of the African community there—as she had felt a strong connection with Africa during her time in Liberia—and the lack of emphasis on the commercial side of music. This photograph was taken in Juan-les-Pins, on the French Riviera, during a jazz festival in 1988.

in his organizational skills. The tour was to include dates at Carnegie Hall and the Newport Jazz Festival, venues where Simone had played very successfully before.

On arrival in New York, though, Simone was taken to court on charges of tax fraud. She was found guilty and sentenced to pay a fine. She felt so nervous and out of sorts in the United States that she fled the country once again—and her promoter had to cancel all of her previously sold-out shows.

In 1978, she moved to Paris, for she viewed the French in a much more positive light than she did the Swiss or, of course, the Americans. "The French are not too bound up in the commercial side of the music industry and you are still admired and popular even if you don't happen to have a record in the pop charts at any particular moment . . . and it has a wonderful African community." (*I Put a Spell on You*, 165) But she was disappointed in France. She had expected, and counted on, bigger crowds and venues. Unable to live on her earnings, she was forced to sell her car and her jewels.

Still, Simone did record one album during this troubled time: In 1977, Creed Taylor, the owner of CTI Records, approached her. Blown away by her performance, he asked her to record for his label, and *Baltimore*, released in 1978, received some glowing reviews. It contained the Randy Newman title track, Quincy Jones's "Everything Must Change," and the Hall and Oates song "Rich Girl." The album earned plaudits from *Rolling Stone*'s Stephen Holden: ". . . [T]he singer runs the emotional gamut from fear, sorrow, and tenderness to a final exhilarating hiss of challenge. . . . *Baltimore* is a stunning comeback by one of the very greatest." (Holden) Despite this and other praise, though, a number of years would pass before Simone's next major album.

The Diva

1978–2003

The tone, the nuances, the implications, the silences, the dynamics, the fortissimos, the pianissimos—all have to do with sound and music, and it's as close to God as I know.

—Nina Simone (quoted in Griffiths)

After CTI released *Baltimore*, Simone spent a few more years living in Paris. The album was warmly received, but Simone wasn't really willing or able to promote it. She played some concerts in Europe and, although she was still living in exile, made some appearances in the United States. She also released *Fodder on Her Wings* in 1982 on the French label Carrère.

Simone's performances continued to be controversial throughout the late 1970s and early 1980s. In a review of one of her 1979 concerts, the African-American music writer Stanley Crouch mentioned that Simone openly criticized the nightclub

Nina's back! In the 1980s, although still living in exile, Simone returned periodically to the United States to perform. She was managing her own career, and the reputation she had earned for canceling shows grew much worse. This did not last too long, though, for she found touring without a manager lonely. She returned to the United States in 1985, and in the following years, she experienced a resurgence of popularity. This photograph is of a concert in New York in June 1985.

management for not paying her on time. Crouch put down her actions, saying, "I suspect that shows of the sort feed the terrible backlash against black people that is again starting to form in this country. . . . Simone played into the hands of those who would, again, disenfranchise us, using incompetence, irresponsibility, and inordinate arrogance as excuses." (Porter, 329)

Writers, too, still spoke of her spotty and unpredictable behavior during shows. David Nathan described how at a performance, "she seemed erratic, and her voice hoarse. She jumped from song to song, from Bob Marley's 'No Woman, No Cry,' to her own 'Pirate Jenny,' and promised she would end the show with 'Young, Gifted, & Black' and 'Where Can I Go Without You.' Instead she delivered 'Baltimore,' 'Everything Must Change,' and 'He Was Too Good to Me.' . . . " (Nathan, 61)

Simone was managing her own career during this time, the early 1980s, and she started to develop a reputation for canceling performances. "Every now and then," she wrote, "I felt a strangeness tugging at the edges of me, and I remembered what had happened to me on the Cosby tour back in the sixties, when I started having visions through overwork. Now I was doing the same sort of tours without any of the staff that I'd had then, and at times it was very hard keeping myself together." (*I Put a Spell on You*, 169) She also confided to David Nathan's sister, Sylvia, for *Blues & Soul* in 1984, that she knew she had developed a reputation as a difficult performer. "They say I'm crazy but they just don't know the real me. . . . No one bothers to look behind the mask. I am a human being, too. I hurt and feel as you but the public sees me as a performer and not a person. . . . I have no one to love and no one to love me. I am alone." (Nathan, 61)

NINA'S BACK

By 1985, Simone finally ended her exile from the United States and moved into a condominium in Los Angeles. She also started working with a new manager, Anthony Sannucci. With Sannucci, Simone recorded her first major album since 1978's *Baltimore*.

Nina's Back, released in 1986 for the label Jungle Freud, seemed to mark another turning point for Simone. The album was praised by both fans and critics. Simone said to Don Heckman of *The Los Angeles Times*, "I'm ready to accept what the public has to give me. And they're giving me a lot. The response I've been getting at all of my programs lately has been fantastic. I wasn't

ready for that before, but now I *want* recognition in this country."
(Phelps, 188) She was ready to achieve a hit. And something
was happening abroad that was going to provide the boost
Simone needed.

Without Simone's knowledge, an advertising company had
decided to use one of her songs to promote Chanel perfumes in
Europe. The track "My Baby Just Cares for Me" from her first
album, "Little Girl Blue" (1958), was being exposed to a brand-
new audience, and they were going crazy for it. When the song
was rereleased in 1987, it quickly became a hit, even though
Simone called it "one of the slightest [songs] I'd ever recorded."
(*I Put a Spell on You*, 170) Although she let everyone know that
she was receiving no royalties for the record, Simone recognized
that this lucky break provided her with a real opportunity to
renew her career. She started playing more across Europe and
making television appearances, and in the process she regained her
confidence. She also hired another agent, Raymond Gonzalez.
Two live recordings bolstered her reputation: Verve's *Live at Vine
Street* (1987) and Essential's *Live at Ronnie Scott's* (1989).

NINA SIMONE'S LAST YEARS

Although Simone still was moving around in the early 1990s,
she seemed to have mellowed. For several years, she lived in
Holland, and then in 1991, she finally settled in Bouc-Bel-Air
in southern France. In her autobiography, she wrote that she
had a "new, more positive attitude." She had a new generation
of fans in Europe, the United States, and Canada, and there were
Simone aficionados all over the globe. David Nathan writes that
at one of her shows around this time, "Nina had been simply
magnificent. The crowd was awestruck. The mere mention of
her name produced a standing ovation, and it became obvious
that the reissue of her music on CDs had generated new interest
in her career." (Nathan, 63)

Also in 1991, Simone published her autobiography,
I Put a Spell on You, which received favorable reviews and

contributed to her resurgence in popularity. Two years later, she signed a contract with Elektra Entertainment, her first deal with an American label since parting ways with RCA in 1974. With Elektra, she released *A Single Woman*, which received very mixed reviews; *The Los Angeles Times* called it "A hit and miss affair." (Phelps, 188) But Simone's star was rising again, strengthened by the inclusion of five of her songs on the soundtrack of the film *Point of No Return* in 1993. She even made an appearance in the movie.

Throughout the 1990s, Simone continued to be as out-spoken and controversial as ever. She made headlines in 1995, for example, when she was fined $5,000 for leaving the scene of a 1993 car accident in France. She also had been charged in France with shooting blank rifle bullets at two teenage boys in 1995. (The boys had been swimming next door while Simone was gardening in her backyard; disturbed by all the noise they were making, she'd responded by firing the gun, injuring one of them.) Simone was given an eight-month suspended jail term and ordered to undergo psychological counseling.

She also maintained her stance against racial inequality in the United States. She canceled gigs, intimidated fans and critics, and subjected her audiences and others to regular outbursts:

> Among divas—a group of performers noted for their ability to be awkward—she stands alone in show-business legend. On a Richter temperament scale from one to ten, she is said to hit at least fifty from time to time. There have been times when she has walked off stage, or not appeared—as on a famous occasion at Ronnie Scott's Club—until one o'clock in the morning. At other times she has not turned up at all, or chewed off the audience's collective ear. At least one writer has suggested that she is especially tough on white male journalists writing for broadsheet newspapers. (Gayford, 1)

"DIFFICULT"

Mike Zwerin, a noted jazz correspondent for London's *International Herald Tribune*, quotes Simone's manager of sixteen years, Raymond Gonzalez, describing a disastrous performance in Pamplona:

> . . . She was having personal problems. Her reputation was in shreds. Based in Geneva, she was working small clubs around Europe. Pamplona was a rare good gig for her. Simone made promoters nervous. She said it was because they did not know how to relate to a creative black woman. They said it was because she was undependable and prone to violence.
>
> . . . She said she would not perform unless she was paid cash in advance. "The promoter was flipping out and I was trying to reason with her. After a big argument she ended up being paid. Then she said to me: 'Now that I have the money, I'm not going to do the concert.'"
>
> It ended up being a nasty concert. She was obviously loaded and she went out of her way to insult the audience. In the confusion, nobody had asked her for a receipt and when the promoter found that out, he fired Gonzalez. The police arrived. There had been complaints of public abuse from the audience. Gonzalez signed the receipt in return for being allowed to get out of town. He rented a car and he and Simone did not speak to each other during the three-hour drive to Biarritz. . . . (Zwerin, 1)

But these incidents had no noticeable effect on her popularity. She was the guest of honor at the Nice Jazz Festival in 1997, the Thessalonika Jazz Festival in 1998, and the Guinness Blues Festival in 1999. Simone's music was anthologized on Verve, Rhino, and RCA. She began to enjoy touring, and she worked her magic on devoted fans in Germany, Brazil, France, Australia, Poland, and the United Kingdom. The rarity of her American appearances only added to her mystique. The music critic Don Shewey opined in *The Village Voice* in 1983 that Simone was "not a pop singer" but "a diva, a hopeless eccentric . . . who has so thoroughly co-mingled her odd talent and brooding temperament that she has turned herself into a force of nature, an exotic creature spied so infrequently that every appearance is legendary." (Shewey, 1)

Toward the end of her life, Simone did become more consistently receptive to American audiences, and she seems to have enjoyed performing in the United States again. In an interview aired on National Public Radio in 2001: "I find that the American audiences haven't left me, and I'm surprised and I'm glad about it. That's a joy. And the bigger the audience, the more I enjoy it. It is my life, not all of it, but I don't have a lover right now. So it is my life." (Spitzer, 1) And the audiences did not leave her; even when her performances fell short of the standards of her earlier years, audiences still called out their love. She had transitioned from performer to phenomenon.

By this time, Lisa, from whom Simone had been estranged, had become a singer and stage actress and achieved considerable critical success. Since then, she has attracted notice for her performance as Mimi in national touring companies of the hit Broadway show *Rent.* She now goes by the stage name "Simone;" as she explained to the magazine *Jet,* "I want to carry on the legacy. There are a lot of things that Mommy didn't get a chance to complete because of the path she chose in regards to the Civil Rights Movement. So I want to complete that journey for her, and hopefully, she will at least be able to travel a little bit of that journey with me." ("Simone, Daughter") In the summer of 1999, Lisa and her mother sang a few duets together at the Guinness Blues Festival in Dublin, Ireland.

Nina Simone also received numerous honors in her last years. In 1998, she was a special guest at Nelson Mandela's eightieth birthday party, and in Dublin, she received an award for lifetime achievement in music. She also received an honorary doctorate in music and humanities, after which she was referred to as *Dr.* Nina Simone. She played in Lebanon, Greece, Switzerland, and the United Kingdom in that year but accepted only a handful of concert dates in the United States.

Simone's performances in 1999 took place mostly in the middle of the year and, again, in the United Kingdom and Ireland. After a hiatus over the winter months, she began 2000 with a series of dates in Brazil; a month after the completion of those, she embarked on a six-month tour of major American cities. She interrupted this tour to perform by invitation at the annual jazz festival in Marciac in southwestern France—a picturesque medieval village of two hundred inhabitants during the off-season and twenty thousand during the festival. The Marciac performance raised eyebrows: Her show, before about six thousand fans, lasted barely an hour, and both her voice and her piano seemed uncertain. Nevertheless, she received the Honorable Musketeer Award from the Compagnie des Mousquetaires d'Armagnac, other recipients of which include John Malkovich, Gabriel Byrne, and Leonardo DiCaprio.

A year after the start of the 2000 tour, in June and July of 2001, Simone launched another month-long tour of the United States. She began with a "kickoff" concert at Constitution Hall in Washington, D.C., then performed at the JVC Jazz Festival at New York's Carnegie Hall before heading to the West Coast for a series of performances in Oregon and California. She closed the tour with several more performances in Chicago, Seattle, and Detroit. A month later, she was back in the United Kingdom, performing at the fifth annual Bishopstock Music Festival in

The death of a legend. Simone settled in southern France in 1991 and spent her final years mostly playing dates in Europe, though she did tour in the United States a few times. She did very little recording, but she continued to play at jazz festivals across the globe, maintaining her uneven reputation but also her legions of fans. Nina Simone died at home in April 2003—a fitting end to a life spent searching for peace. Her daughter, Lisa Celeste (known as Simone), walked in the funeral procession in Carry-le-Rouet; hundreds of mourners attended the service.

Exeter; according to one observer, she could "barely walk these days," "[h]er speaking voice . . . [was] deep and slow and slurred," and she asked whether Devon were in London. Nevertheless, "[H]er singing voice [was] deep and crisp and even." (Aizlewood, 1) At the Carnegie Hall concert, she "had to be helped to the stage, and was later seen sitting backstage in a wheelchair." (Moody, 1)

Nina Simone died on Monday, April 21, 2003, at her home in Carry-le-Rouet, France. She was seventy years old and had been a giant in the music industry for forty years. Hundreds attended her funeral, which was held four days later. The service opened with Jacques Brel's "Ne Me Quitte Pas"—"Don't Leave Me"—one of Simone's most heartbreaking standards. Separate services were held in New York and in her hometown of Tryon before her ashes were scattered over Africa.

Irascible, unmanageable, uneven, and utterly transcendent, Simone left a legacy all her own. Beyond all the jazzy and heart-breaking renditions she had given to the world—songs that still, even decades later, carry their listeners through long nights—she had lent a strong and public voice to the black experience in the United States. More than that of any other singer of the time, Simone's work expressed the great frustration of the African-American heritage, and she delivered her message in a way that millions could understand. She was angry with the United States, angry enough to live in voluntary exile; but her deep dissatisfaction with American race relations was really a kind of disappointed love. The extreme devotion she inspired in her fans was due less to her social activism than to her sadness—for Nina Simone sang the pain of not belonging.

1933   Eunice Kathleen Waymon, later Nina Simone, is born on February 21 in Tryon, North Carolina.

1936–1937   Learns to play some hymns on the family organ by ear.

1939–1945   Studies with Muriel Massinovitch, funded first by Mrs. Miller, her mother's employer, then by the Eunice Waymon Fund.

1945–1949   Attends the Allen High School for Girls in Asheville, North Carolina; studies with Joyce Carrol.

1950–1951   Attends Juilliard School of Music and studies with Dr. Carl Friedberg.

1951   Is denied admission to the Curtis Institute of Music.

1952–1954   Studies with Vladimir Sokhaloff; works as an accompanist at Arlene Smith Studio in Philadelphia; teaches private lessons.

1954   Begins performing at the Midtown Bar and Grill, Atlantic City, New Jersey; first known recording is made in Philadelphia.

1956   Begins performing in clubs in Philadelphia.

1957   Performs in supper clubs in New York City and Upstate New York; signs with Bethlehem Records and begins recording.

1958   *Little Girl Blue* (Bethlehem Records); marries Don Ross.

1959   Signs with Colpix Records (until 1964) and releases *The Amazing Nina Simone* (Colpix); Bethlehem releases *Nina Simone and Her Friends*; "I Loves You Porgy" reaches the top twenty on U.S. pop charts; performs at Town Hall, New York, on September 12; divorces Don Ross.

1960   *Nina Simone at Town Hall* (Colpix); appears on *The Ed Sullivan Show* in September.

1961   Marries Andrew Stroud on December 4; *Nina Simone at Newport* and *Forbidden Fruit* (both Colpix); travels to Nigeria and performs in concerts with Langston Hughes, James Baldwin, and others with the American Society of African Culture.

1962   Husband Stroud becomes Simone's manager; *Nina Simone at the Village Gate* and *Nina Simone Sings Ellington!* (both Colpix); daughter, Lisa Celeste Stroud, is born on September 12.

1963   In September, composes "Mississippi Goddam" in response to the murder of civil rights leader Medgar Evers and a church bombing that claimed the lives of four young girls; *Nina Simone at Carnegie Hall* (Colpix); begins performing at various SNCC and CORE benefits.

1964   *Folksy Nina* (Colpix); signs with Philips Records (until 1967); *In Concert* and *Broadway-Blues-Ballads* (both Philips).

1965   Performs at the Selma-to-Montgomery March; tours Europe, including dates at the Montreux Jazz Festival and in Antibes; *I Put a Spell on You* (Philips).

1966   *Nina Simone with Strings* (Colpix); *Let It All Out, Wild Is the Wind,* and *Pastel Blues* (all Philips); signs with RCA Records (until 1974); begins touring with Bill Cosby.

1967   *High Priestess of Soul* (Philips); *Nina Simone Sings the Blues* and *Silk & Soul* (both RCA).

1968   Martin Luther King, Jr., is murdered on April 4; begins another tour of Europe and performs again at Montreux.

1969 *A Very Rare Evening* (PM); *'Nuff Said, Nina Simone and Piano!*, and *To Love Somebody* (all RCA); Philips releases *The Best of Nina Simone* (from earlier recordings).

1970 Moves to Barbados with daughter, Lisa; has affair with Prime Minister Earl Barrow; *Black Gold* (RCA).

1971 Divorces Andy Stroud; *Here Comes the Sun* (RCA).

1972 *Emergency Ward!* (RCA).

1974 RCA releases its last album with Nina Simone, *It Is Finished*; Simone moves to Liberia with Lisa.

1976 Simone and Lisa move to Switzerland.

1978 *Baltimore* (Columbia); Simone is tried for having withheld taxes seven years earlier and ordered to pay a fine.

1980 Records tracks in Montreal that are released by the jazz label Enja Records as *The Rising Sun Collection*.

1982 *Fodder on My Wings* (Carrère), recorded in Paris in January.

1984 *Live at Ronnie Scott's* (The Collection), recorded in London in November.

1985 *Nina's Back* (VPI).

1987 *My Baby Just Cares for Me* is rereleased in the United Kingdom and becomes a hit; *Live at Vine Street* and *Let It Be Me* (both Verve); *Live & Kickin'* (Singleton).

1991 Simone's cowritten autobiography, *I Put a Spell on You,* is published.

1993 Appears in film *Point of No Return*; five of her songs are included on the soundtrack; *A Single Woman* (Elektra).

1995	Simone is arrested and fined after shooting blank bullets into yard of two teenage boys; she is also fined for leaving the scene of an accident that occurred in 1993.
1994–1999	Does not record; tours in Europe, playing at numerous jazz festivals.
2000, 2001	Tours mainly in the United States.
2003	Dies on April 21 in Carry-le-Rouet in southern France.

Works by Nina Simone

Little Girl Blue (Jazz as Played in an Exclusive Side Street), 1958

The Amazing Nina Simone, 1959

Nina Simone and Her Friends, 1959

Nina Simone at Town Hall, 1960

Nina Simone at Newport, 1961

Forbidden Fruit, 1961

At the Village Gate, 1962

Nina Simone Sings Ellington!, 1962

Nina's Choice, 1963

At Carnegie Hall, 1963

Folksy Nina, 1964

In Concert, 1964

Broadway-Blues-Ballads, 1964

I Put a Spell on You, 1965

With Strings, 1966

Pastel Blues, 1966

Let It All Out, 1966

Wild Is the Wind, 1966

High Priestess of Soul, 1967

Nina Simone Sings the Blues, 1967

Silk & Soul, 1967

'Nuff Said, 1969

Nina Simone and Piano!, 1969

To Love Somebody, 1969

Black Gold, 1970

Here Comes the Sun, 1971

Emergency Ward!, 1972

It Is Finished, 1974

Baltimore, 1978

Fodder on My Wings, 1982

Nina's Back!, 1985

Live & Kickin', 1987

Let It Be Me, 1987

A Single Woman, 1993

Bibliography

Aizlewood, John. "Reviews: Nina Simone." *The Guardian* (August 28, 2001), available online at *www.guardian.co.uk/arts/reviews/story/0,11712,704146,00.html.*

Bardin, Brentley. "Simone Says." *Details* (January 1997). Quoted at Boscarol, "Interviews," *www.boscarol.com/nina/html/manual/interview/details.html.*

Boscarol, Mauro. "The Nina Simone Web." *www.boscarol.com/nina/index.htm.*

Brennan, Luann, ed. *Contemporary Musicians.* Vol. 11. Gale Research, 1997.

Caras, Roger. *The Amazing Nina Simone* (CD liner notes). Colpix, 1959.

Erlewine, Michael, et al., eds. *The All Music Guide to Jazz.* Miller Freeman, 1996.

Gavin, James. *Broadway-Blues-Ballads* (CD liner notes). Verve, 1993 rerelease.

Gayford, Martin. "Difficult? She Just Hates Showbiz." *The Daily Telegraph* (London) (December 14, 1998). Quoted at Boscarol, "Magazine Articles," *www.boscarol.com/nina/html/articles/telegraph.html.*

Gilmore, Jennifer. "Nina Simone." Salon.com (June 20, 2000). Available through the archives of Salon.com at *archive.salon.com/people/bc/2000/06/20/simone/.*

Goldblatt, Burt. *Newport Jazz Festival: An Illustrated History.* Doubleday, 1977.

Griffiths, Emma. "Tribute to the High Priestess of Soul, Nina Simone." *The 7:30 Report* (Australian Broadcasting). Available online at *www.abc.net.au/7.30/content/2003/s837818.htm.*

Harrington, Richard. "Nina Simone: A Voice to Be Reckoned With." *The Washington Post* (April 22, 2003):C01.

Holden, Stephen. Review of *Baltimore. Rolling Stone* (August 10, 1978).

Jenkins, Willard. "Nina Simone, 1933–2003." Africana.com (April 22, 2003), *www.africana.com/articles/daily/mu20030422nina.asp.*

Kosner, Edward. *The New York Post* (March 10, 1961).

Lanker, Brian. *I Dream a World: Portraits of Black Women Who Changed America.* Stewart, Tabori, and Chang, 1999.

Moody, Nekesa Mumbi. "Nina Simone Dies at 70." Associated Press (April 21, 2003).

Nathan, David. *The Soulful Divas: Personal Portraits of Over a Dozen Divas, from Nina Simone, Aretha Franklin, and Diana Ross to Patti Labelle, Whitney Houston, and Janet Jackson.* Billboard, 1999.

O'Brien, Lucy. *She Bop: The Definitive History of Women, Rock, Pop, and Soul II.* Continuum, 2002.

Phelps, Shirelle, ed. *Contemporary Black Biography.* Vol. 15. Gale Research, 1997.

Porter, Eric. *What Is This Thing Called Jazz?* University of California Press, 2002.

Powell, Alison. "The American Soul of Nina Simone." *Interview* (January 1997). Quoted at Boscarol, "Interviews," *www.boscarol.com/nina/html/manual/interview/interview.html.*

Roland, Paul, ed. *Jazz Singers: The Great Song Stylists in Their Own Words.* Watson-Guptill, 2000.

Shewey, Don. "Le Petit Mort de Nina Simone." *The Village Voice* (June 21, 1983). Available online at *www.donshewey.com/music_articles/nina_simone.html.*

Siegel, Joel E. *High Priestess of Soul* (CD liner notes). Mercury, 1990 rerelease.

"Simone, Daughter of Nina Simone, Wins Rave Reviews for Her Performance in *Rent.*" *Jet* (March 9, 1998).

Simone, Nina, with Stephen Cleary. *I Put A Spell on You: The Autobiography of Nina Simone.* Pantheon, 1991; reprinted by Da Capo, 1993.

Spitzer, Nick. Interview with Nina Simone. *Weekly Edition* (National Public Radio) (July 21, 2001). Sound file available online at *www.npr.org/programs/weed/archives/2001/jul/010722.weed.html.*

Ward, Brian. *Just My Soul Responding: Rhythm and Blues, Black Consciousness, and Race Relations.* University of California Press, 1998.

Wilson, John S. Interview with Nina Simone. *The New York Times* (October 22, 1960).

———. Review of Nina Simone concert at Town Hall. *The New York Times* (September 15, 1959).

Zwerin, Mike. "Nina Simone: An Appreciation." Culturekiosque.com (May 2, 2003), *www.culturekiosque.com/jazz/portrait/ninasimone.html.*

Further Reading

Books

Erlewine, Michael, et al., eds. *The All Music Guide to Jazz.* Miller Freeman, 1996.

Garland, Paul. *The Sound of Soul.* Regney, 1969.

George-Warren, Holly, and Patricia Romanowski, eds. *The* Rolling Stone *Encyclopedia of Rock and Roll.* Fireside, 2001.

Gottheimer, Josh, ed. *Ripples of Hope: Great American Civil Rights Speeches.* BasicCivitas Books, 2003.

Gregory, Hugh. *Soul Music: A−Z.* Da Capo, 1995.

King, Martin Luther, and Coretta Scott King. *I Have a Dream.* Scholastic Trade, 1997.

Lanker, Brian. *I Dream a World: Portraits of Black Women Who Changed America.* Stewart, Tabori, and Chang, 1999.

Nathan, David. *The Soulful Divas: Personal Portraits of Over a Dozen Divas, from Nina Simone, Aretha Franklin, and Diana Ross to Patti Labelle, Whitney Houston, and Janet Jackson.* Billboard, 1999.

Parks, Rosa, and Gregory J. Reed, *Dear Mrs. Parks: A Dialogue With Today's Youth.* Lee & Low Books, 1996.

Ribeiro, Myra. *The Assassination of Medgar Evers.* Rosen, 2002.

Williams, Richard. *Nina Simone: Don't Let Me Be Misunderstood.* Cannongate, 2004.

Websites

The Nina Simone Web
www.boscarol.com/nina/index.htm
The premiere resource on all things Nina, including all her songs, albums, and recording sessions, as well as her life and the people in it.

Graeme's Nina Simone Page
www.seercom.com/bluto/nina/

The Official Site of Billie Holiday
www.cmgww.com/music/holiday/

U.S. Library of Congress: African-American Odyssey: The Civil Rights Era
memory.loc.gov/ammem/aaohtml/exhibit/aopart9.html

U.S. Department of State: Information USA: Civil Rights: Overviews
usinfo.state.gov/usa/infousa/crights/overview.htm

Western Michigan University Department of Political Science: Timeline
of the American Civil Rights Movement
www.wmich.edu/politics/mlk/

University of Southern Mississippi: Civil Rights Documentation Project
www-dept.usm.edu/~mcrohb/

We Shall Overcome: Historic Places of the Civil Rights Movement
www.cr.nps.gov/nr/travel/civilrights/index.htm

The 1963 Birmingham Church Bombing
www.4littlegirls.com

Index

Index

Index

Credits

page:

13: Associated Press, AP/Mark Lennihan
18: © Bettmann/CORBIS
21: © Hulton-Deutsch Collection/CORBIS
26: © Nubar Alexanian/CORBIS
29: © Bettmann/CORBIS
33: Associated Press, AP
38: Library of Congress, LC-G412-9288-001
41: Associated Press, AP
45: © Hulton/Archive by Getty Images, Inc.
50: © Reuters NewMedia Inc./CORBIS
53: © Hulton-Deutsch Collection/CORBIS
55: © AFP/CORBIS

65: © Hulton/Archive by Getty Images, Inc.
68: © Bettmann/CORBIS
73: © Daniel Lainé/CORBIS
80: Associated Press, AP
85: © Bettmann/CORBIS
89: © AFP/CORBIS
94: © Hulton-Deutsch Collection /CORBIS
99: Associated Press, AP
106: © AFP/CORBIS
109: Associated Press, AP/Rene Perez
116: Associated Press, AP/Claude Paris

Cover: © Hulton/Archive by Getty Images, Inc.

Contributors

Kerry Acker is a freelance writer and editor based in Brooklyn, New York. Her previous books include *The Kids Fun-Filled Encyclopedia* and *Backyard Animals* (both published by Kidsbooks, Inc.), *Everything You Need to Know About the Goth Scene* (Rosen Publishing), and *The Millennium Journal* (Andrews McMeel). She holds a bachelor's degree in English literature and Spanish from the College of the Holy Cross in Worcester, Massachusetts.

Congresswoman Betty McCollum (Minnesota, Fourth District) is the second woman from Minnesota ever to have been elected to Congress. Since the start of her first term of office in 2000, she has worked diligently to protect the environment and to expand access to health care, and she has been an especially strong supporter of education and women's health care. She holds several prominent positions in the House Democratic Caucus and enjoys the rare distinction of serving on three House Committees at once. In 2001, she was appointed to represent the House Democrats on the National Council on the Arts, the advisory board of the National Endowment for the Arts.